Joy to the world

JOY TO THE WORLD

Communicating the Gospel of Christ

Arthur Blessitt

Marshalls

Marshall Paperbacks
Marshall Morgan & Scott
1 Bath Street, London EC1V 9LB

First published by Marshall Morgan & Scott 1982

ISBN: 0 551 00963 2

Phototypeset by Input Typesetting Ltd, London

Printed in Great Britain by
Richard Clay (The Chaucer Press) Ltd,
Bungay, Suffolk

INTRODUCTION

One day when I was in college I went to the post office. As I walked in, I saw a poster on the wall. It was a picture of Uncle Sam. He had his finger pointing out and under his finger were the words, 'I want you.' As I read those words, my heart was suddenly pierced with God's call. I noticed something strange, for each time I moved, the finger was still pointing and the eyes were still looking. It was the artist's way of making it a personal call. I realized that Jesus Christ was saying to me, 'I want you! I want you as long as you're standing in front of the cross.' And he is saying to all Christians that He wants you. He wants you living in victory. He wants you everywhere declaring the good news. He wants you loving the poor, clothing the naked. He wants you to be His example in this world. And to those of you who have never given your life to Jesus, He is saying, 'I want you!' He wants you in His family. He wants you to be in heaven. He wants to give you His Holy Spirit. He wants to forgive your sins. He wants to give you a new life. He wants to put your life together. Isn't that good news! God wants you.

God has chosen us as His witnesses. He has chosen us as His ambassadors so that we may communicate the love of God. We are the only way the world will know. God has not chosen to engrave His message in the sky, God has chosen you and me as His ambassadors. And it is our privilege to communicate and share the glorious message of Jesus Christ. He has entrusted redemption to us. It is the greatest compliment in all the world that God has enough confidence in us to use us as His witnesses. The Bible says, 'And how can they believe in the one of whom they have not heard? And how can they hear without someone preaching to them?' (Rom. 10.14).

Jesus said, 'Therefore go and make disciples of all nations' (Mt. 28.19). We are to make disciples of people everywhere. We have been chosen by God to deliver a message. We've not just been saved to escape the flames of hell or to enjoy a paradise of golden streets. No, we have been redeemed by God to know Him, and to experience His love and to convey His message of love to people who have lost their direction, who have not come to understand this. And so, God has entrusted Himself in my flesh.

The Bible says, 'Do you not know that your body is a temple of the Holy Spirit, who is in you, whom you have received from God? You are not your own; you were bought at a price. Therefore honour God with your body' (1 Cor. 6.19, 20). God wants our bodies to be His tabernacle. He wants us to be His witnesses, delivering the message of life everywhere. Isn't that a wonderful privilege? How would you feel if you were to take a message from the President to the leaders of another nation? You would feel pride, and yet humility. You would feel honour, and maybe you would feel a sense of unworthiness. But God, the Almighty King of Kings and Lord of Lords has said that He wants Mary, John, Mr. Smith, Mr. Jones, to go to your next-door neighbours and let them know that He loves them. He's going to use you as His witness to those who are hungry, as you feed them, and they'll know He cares. To those who don't understand it, you'll explain the Bible so they'll know that He is interested in communicating with them. God has chosen you. And you can't fail. How can you say no? How can you say, I won't go? God is pointing, God is calling. You accept that call and go for God.

DAY 1

For the next few weeks I'm going to be looking at the most wonderful person in all the world, and that is Jesus. Now, as I share about Him, I want you to understand this. Many of us, as we witness, talk about giving our lives to Christ, but we're always talking about living the Christian life, about reading the Bible, about repentance – that's talking about the things we shouldn't do. But many of us talk about the things we should do. I find that a lot of us never really concentrate on Jesus. It is Jesus who is the Saviour. It is not a plan that saved you. It is not a way of life, because Jesus is the way, He is the truth and He is the life. I want to encourage you to talk about Jesus.

Who is Jesus? I could write for hours and hours about Him. I want to share a capsule of thought about who Jesus Christ is. Jesus Christ is God. He is God who came in the flesh and was conceived in the womb of Mary by the Holy Spirit. When He died upon the cross and shed His blood, it was the blood of God that was shed for the remission of sin. That is why only through Jesus Christ can people be saved.

He was born in a manger stall, and was identified at His birth with the poor and the homeless. Most of the people of this world are poor, and don't have an adequate diet and Jesus Christ understood. He was born in that sort of condition. As a young child, He had to cross the Sinai Desert with His parents, all the way through to Egypt, because Herod threatened and sought to kill Him. He lived as a refugee. He came back and grew up in Nazareth. He was baptized by John. He went into the wilderness and fasted and prayed for forty days. He began to preach and teach and work miracles. Never a man spake as He. No one has ever done the things that Jesus Christ did. Unique in all of history, He is the Son of God, the Saviour of the world. He loved the poor, He loved the drunkards and the prostitutes. He said, 'Come to me, all you who are weary and burdened, and I will give you rest' (Mt. 11.28). He went into the homes of the rich. He cared for people in every circumstance. When you share Jesus Christ show who He is. He said, 'When I am lifted up from the earth, I will draw all men to myself' (Jn. 12.32). Sometimes people don't want to hear about your church, but everywhere I go I find people who want to hear about Jesus.

DAY 2

Continuing with the subject from yesterday, Jesus Christ. Jesus lived in the world. He walked along the roadside, He sat down in the grass, He was weary, He cried. He loved people, He was hungry, He was thirsty and yet he was God. When people heard Him speak, they said nobody had ever spoken like that. They had heard prophets, but they had never heard anyone like Jesus. They had never seen anyone live the way Jesus lived. He actually loved the people. When Hc was around lepers, He touched them. When He was around prostitutes, He let one wash His feet. When He was around the poor, He gave them something to eat. Jesus Christ cared and He loved. Then the day came when Jesus was in the Garden of Gethsemane, and He prayed, 'My Father, if it is possible, may this cup be taken from me. Yet not as I will, but as you will' (Mt. 26.39). Jesus Christ willingly gave Himself before Pilate and the angry crowd, and let them lead Him away. Then He hung on the cross, crucified.

I have walked for many years carrying a huge cross; I've been spat upon, and I've seen a lot of bitterness. Jesus Christ really suffered for us. Scourged and nailed to the cross, He not only suffered physically, but He carried our sins too. That's the difference. Many people have been crucified, but only Christ died for our sins. As His head was slumped in death, He cried out, 'It is finished' (Jn. 19.30). The way of salvation was paid for through the blood of Jesus. When you witness, be sure to share that the blood of Jesus Christ is what cleanses us from all sin.

Then on the third day, Jesus was resurrected, triumphant! Hallelujah! He is alive and living. He ascended unto the Father, and two angels said, 'This same Jesus, who has been taken from you into heaven, will come back in the same way you have seen him go into heaven' (Acts 1.11). One day, one moment, the sound of the trumpet shall ring and the shout of the archangel shall be heard and Jesus Christ shall descend from heaven, and all those who are ready and prepared will be caught up to meet Him in the air! Are you ready?

DAY 3

Now I'm going to look at how Jesus shared the message of truth with a different person in different circumstances. There was a man named Nicodemus, he was a good, moral man and he was a leader. And he came to Jesus and said,

‘We know you are a teacher who has come from God. For no-one could perform the miraculous signs you are doing if God were not with him’ (Jn. 3.2). This man knew that here was a miraculous person; he saw miracles in the life of Jesus. But then Jesus answered him back with a straight shot. Here I’m looking at how Christ shared. Nicodemus said something complimentary to Jesus and He said, ‘Unless a man is born again, he cannot see the Kingdom of God’ (Jn. 3.3). Jesus always spoke straight, but lovingly, kindly and clearly. There was no way to misunderstand Him. He said that you need a new birth, or you’ll never see the Kingdom of God. And then Nicodemus asked how could a man go back into his mother’s womb and be born a second time. Here was a man thinking wordly, materialistic thoughts, and Jesus continues to deal with him spiritually. He said, ‘Unless a man is born of water and the Spirit, he cannot enter the Kingdom of God’ (Jn. 3.5). Jesus took this man who was thinking of earthly and physical things and presented spiritual truths to him, and He kept comparing them. He didn’t rebuke him but He changed him. He transformed him to realize that there was a spiritual dimension in his life.

Now let’s look at what Jesus said to him. ‘I tell you the truth, we speak of what we know, and we testify what we have seen, but still you do not accept our testimony’ (Jn. 3.11). Jesus was speaking of that which He knew to be the truth. Share the message of life simply and clearly.

Jesus then goes on to explain the full gospel to Nicodemus. 'For God so loved the world that He gave His one and only Son, that whoever believes in Him shall not perish but have eternal life. For God did not send His Son into the world to condemn the world, but to save the world through Him' (Jn. 3.16, 17). That was Christ's witness to Nicodemus. He explained the full gospel, the gospel of repentance; of us turning from an old life to live a new life; a new birth; and then He shared how He was coming to give Himself for our sins and that in Him we have eternal life. Jesus was saying that He had not come to condemn him, but that if he believed in Him, he may be saved. In other words, 'I've come to deliver you the good news'.

Now as you witness, I challenge you today to witness with the love and the understanding of Christ. If people say something to you which is earthly, change it and bring Jesus Christ to them and share the truth of salvation and love of Jesus.

DAY 4

Today I'm going to look at how Jesus talked to a woman in His everyday life. The Bible says that Jesus was making a journey, and as He was travelling, He came to a place where there was a well of water, and He was weary. The disciples went into town to get food and Jesus sat by the well. A woman approached Him and He asked her a question. He said, 'Will you give me a drink?' (Jn. 4.7), and they started to talk.

Now, there are several things about the witnessing life of Jesus that I want to note. It was at the end of a typical day, He was exhausted and she came up and He began to talk to her. He initiated a conversation and it had to do with water. Now, many of you go down to the launderette; you're at a petrol station; you're doing various jobs around the house or business, in your everyday life – and you're in touch with people all the time. So was Jesus. He took advantage of the people that were around Him to share the message of salvation.

As Jesus began to talk with the woman, she was astounded that He, a Jew, would talk to her, a Samaritan. This had to do with racial prejudice. And Jesus said, 'If you knew the gift of God and who it is that asks you for a drink, you would have asked Him and He would have given you living water' (Jn. 4.10). Here you see a conversation where Jesus heightens her curiosity, 'If you knew. . .'. Sometimes when you're in your place of business or work, or whatever, and you're happy and joyous and you say, 'Isn't it a wonderful day!' and someone replies, 'I don't know what's so wonderful about it'. You can say, 'Because of God's gift of eternal life, because of the happiness that Jesus gives.'

Christ was sharing with the Samaritan woman about how she could have living water and He said to her again, 'Everyone who drinks this water will be thirsty again, but whoever drinks the water I give him will become in him a spring of water, welling up to eternal life' (Jn. 4.13, 14). Isn't it wonderful to see how once again Jesus took the physical and brought out the spiritual impact. The physical water, the spiritual water – the physical water satisfies your body, the spiritual water, Jesus, satisfies your soul.

The woman replied, 'Give me this water', then Jesus said, 'Go, call your husband.' He dealt with sin and repentance here. And she said, 'I have no husband'. He said, 'You are right when you say you have no husband. The fact is, you have had five husbands, and the man you now have is not your husband' (Jn. 4. 17, 18). She was under conviction, but He dealt with her sin in love. Then she said, 'I know that Messiah is coming. When He comes, He will explain everything to us'. Then Jesus declared, 'I who speak to you am He' (Jn. 4.25, 26). Jesus announced that He was the Saviour and in that instant she believed. She dropped her water pot and started running into the city. Jesus took her from her interest in the water, through her prejudice, to eternal life. And you can share Jesus Christ with somebody today, and communicate that He's the way, the truth and the life.

DAY 5

Yesterday, I discussed the woman at the well and how Jesus met her, shared the truth with her, and how she received Him as her Saviour. Now today I want you to notice the change that took place in this woman's life. The Bible says that immediately after she had believed, 'Leaving her water jar, the woman went back to the town and said to the people, "Come, see a man who told me everything I ever did. Could this be the Christ?" ' (Jn. 4.28, 29). Hallelujah! Here was a woman who was living in sin, an adulteress, probably the town prostitute, and she met Jesus at the well, she came to believe that He was the Messiah in one conversation. And she dropped the water pot she was carrying and went running back into the city.

Here was a woman changed through her faith in Jesus Christ, and who ran back to the city to speak to the men. Now sometimes we're taught that women shouldn't witness to men or men shouldn't witness to women, but Jesus changed this woman's life and she ran into the city and she talked to the men. Have you ever wondered why she went to the men? I believe it's because the women wouldn't have anything to do with her, and the men were the ones who had been her companions. She went back to those who she had sinned with, and said, 'Come, see a man who told me everything I ever did'. No wonder a big crowd turned up; she told them about a man who knew everything that every one of them had ever done. That would draw a crowd anywhere, wouldn't it?

The people of the city ran out to listen to Jesus and the Bible says, 'Many of the Samaritans from that town believed in Him because of the woman's testimony' (Jn. 4.39). They came out and listened to Jesus and believed in Him just because of what He said, and they asked Him to stay, and Jesus stayed in the town two days. Because a prostitute was converted and began immediately to witness, they had a two day revival with Jesus.

Several things about witnessing can be learnt here. When we receive Jesus, our hearts are changed right away. Secondly, we should start witnessing at once. Thirdly, we should witness to the people we know, those whom we've sinned with perhaps. Some of you say that you've done so many bad things that maybe you should move to another town. Well, here is this woman going back to those with whom she had sinned. And finally, we see this woman with no training, become an effective witness, with people believing in Jesus because of what she said.

DAY 6

Now as I continue to look at the woman who was converted at the well, who went into the city and witnessed, and the men who came out, I want you to notice something about the disciples. The Bible tells us that the disciples had gone to get food from the same city that this woman went into. And as the men were buying groceries, Jesus sat by the well and began to witness to this woman. As the disciples came away from the city, they had no revival. They hadn't witnessed. God had saved nobody. Jesus had been training his disciples but they had failed on the job. On their return, they pressed Him to eat, 'Rabbi, eat something.' But Jesus said, 'I have food to eat that you know nothing about'. The disciples were puzzled, 'Could someone have brought Him food!' and Jesus said, 'My food is to do the will of Him who sent me and to finish His work' (Jn. 4.32–34).

Jesus' desire was to witness. It was His spiritual food. Many of us are as blind as those disciples as we go about our daily routine. We never witness for Jesus, but this woman went into the city and she witnessed, she preached to the men and the whole city came out. A saved prostitute brought revival. The disciples had gone in and bought groceries but had no results. And that's tragic. Many of you have been trained; you know the Bible; you've gone to Sunday School; to church, and yet you're not productive. God wants to use you. You say now is not the time, but Jesus said, 'Do you not say, "Four months more and then the harvest?" I tell you, open your eyes and look at the fields! They are ripe for harvest' (Jn. 4.35). You need to get out there and let your desire be to share Jesus.

DAY 7

Today, I'm going to look at lady who received Jesus Christ as her Lord. I'm going to comment on how Christ dealt with a critical situation. You find the story in John chapter 8.

Jesus was teaching and a crowd had gathered to hear Him. Then Jesus' critics came along bringing a woman, literally dragging her, and threw her at the feet of Jesus. The woman, they said, had been caught in the act of adultery. Now the Law of Moses said they should stone her to death because she was an adulteress, but this would bring them into conflict with the Roman authorities. Whatever Jesus said, He was caught. But led by the Spirit and by the Father, instead of condemning or condoning her for anything, He simply leaned over and wrote in the dirt, and his critics must have stood there confused. Here's a woman thrown at His feet, with a crowd looking on, and a group wanting to have her killed. What will you say Jesus? And Jesus looked up and said to them, 'If any one of you is without sin, let him be the first to throw a stone at her,' (Jn. 8.7), and then Jesus bent over and started to mark with his finger again. After a few moments, 'those who heard began to go away one at a time, the older ones first, until only Jesus was left, with the woman still standing there' (Jn. 8.9).

Here is Christ gently, in love, looking up at this one woman, when all the critics had left because they had certainly sinned. Now as you look at Jesus, He looks at this woman. She must have looked up into His eyes, seeing the purity and the holiness, here was God in the flesh. And she a sinner, an adulteress, and Jesus said, 'Woman, where are they? Has no-one condemned you?' 'No-one Sir,' she said. And Jesus said, 'Then neither do I condemn you. Go now and leave your life of sin' (Jn. 8.10, 11).

Isn't this marvellous? Just to realize right here that Jesus Christ loves. See the gentleness that reached out from Him. As He loved this woman – He did not condemn her in bitterness. Many of us in our witnessing are like knives, slashing and stabbing at those who've done wrong, but Jesus, He knew she was condemned and she knew she was condemned. And yet, somehow, in the midst of that condemnation she came to experience His love. As you witness today, in your witness, let it be a witness of love. The world is condemned enough, it needs the good news of life and love and salvation. This is what this lady needed and Jesus loved her. And by saying, 'go on your way, sin no more, I am the light of the world, trust me', she received Him as her Lord and began to live a new life.

DAY 8

I'm still looking at the life of Jesus, trying to understand how He witnessed, how He loved, how He shared, and that's the same type of witness we want to be, and that He wants us to be. Today I'm looking in Luke chapter 19. Jesus was going into Jericho and as He was walking along, suddenly He looked up in a tree and there was a short guy sitting up in the top. He knew the man's heart, and He knew that the man wanted to know Him. He wanted to see Jesus, but he was too short to see from the huge crowd that had gathered. Now, we'll notice a beautiful thing about Jesus when the Bible says, 'He looked up and said to him, "Zacchaeus, come down immediately. I must stay at your house today" ' (Lk. 19.5). To me, these are some of the most thrilling words Jesus spoke, because here He called a man to Himself. He invited a man to know Him; to trust Him and to come down to be with Him. Jesus was saying that He was coming to Zacchaeus' house, to eat with him and visit him, to be his friend. And the man came down and received Him joyfully.

Jesus went into the man's house but the crowd began to criticize Him because He was the guest of a man who was a sinner. Then look at Zacchaeus, 'But Zacchaeus stood up and said to the Lord, "Look, Lord! Here and now I give half of my possessions to the poor, and if I have cheated anybody out of anything, I will pay back four times the amount" ' (Lk. 19.8). Here's the transformation of Christ and this is the kind of witness that we need to be.

We need to be willing to be the friends of people who other people are unfriendly to. If anybody loves in this world, it should be Jesus' followers. But often it's the Christian pointing and condemning and judging, but Jesus didn't judge, He didn't condemn. What He did was to go into the man's house and say, 'I want to eat with you, I want to be your friend.' That's the kind of witness that God wants you to be. Maybe there's a friend of yours who you need to call up and invite to your home for dinner. Maybe there's a friend who has asked you to go to their house, then go and eat with them. Maybe some of your friends are gathering in places where you don't normally go, maybe you should go there and answer the call, the invitation they have given you and bear witness of Jesus. I challenge you to take advantage of every opportunity you get in the world, and share Jesus Christ. And let's get out with the gospel and go, go, go!

DAY 9

I'm now ready to look at something which Jesus did that was unique and very special, and I believe it will help many of us Christians to witness more effectively, in realizing how instantly a person can be converted and then how quickly they can witness for the Lord. You'll find the story that I'm sharing about today, in Mark chapter 5. Jesus had sailed across the Sea of Galilee to an area called the Gadarenes, and living there was a man who was really insane. He was filled with demonic spirits; he tore at himself, and people tried to chain him but he would break the chains; he lived in caves and tombs and went about as a wild man, running naked in the mountains.

Jesus landed on the shore and the man saw Him, and came running toward Him, and the demons in him cried out because Jesus said, 'Come out of this man, you evil spirit!' He started to cast the demons out and the man begged Him repeatedly, 'not to send them out of the area'. And then the demons begged Jesus, 'Send us among the pigs;' (Mk. 5.8–12). And these demon spirits were cast into the pigs, and the pigs ran over the cliff edge and plunged into the sea. Then we read that many came to Jesus to see the man who was possessed with the devil, and saw him 'sitting there, dressed and in his right mind; and they were afraid' (Mk. 5.15).

You see, Jesus changed his life. In a moment, he was set free, he was a new person, he put clothes on, he was sitting at the feet of Jesus, listening as Jesus talked and preached. But the people were afraid because Jesus had cast these demons out of the man, and had caused the pigs to leap off the cliff. In other words, Jesus cost them some money because the demons went into the pigs. And the people urged Him to move on. Everybody was against Jesus except this one man, and he begged Jesus that he might go with him. But Jesus said, 'Go home to your family and tell them how much the Lord has done for you, and how He has had mercy on you'

(Mk. 5.19). Isn't this marvellous! Here was Jesus with this man set free and the man, wanting to go with Him, to learn from Him, to be one of the followers. And Jesus, refusing to take him, but telling him to go to his friends, who had seen him in his former rage – naked and tearing himself. Jesus asked him to go and tell the people what great things He had done; he was to be Jesus' witness. And Jesus left him alone.

The Bible records that several months later, Jesus went back to the country and all the people received Him. Why? Because that man had been out there witnessing. Let's look at the witness of Jesus. He proclaimed the gospel, set the man at liberty and sent him witnessing right after he was saved. When you lead somebody to Jesus, you need to encourage them right then to tell their wife or their children or their parents or their friends about Jesus. Let's all get out into the world and spread the good news of Jesus!

DAY 10

By now, Jesus had been travelling for some time with the disciples from town to town. One day they ended up near Caesarea, Philippi. They may have been sitting around the fire, after eating, I don't know the circumstances, but they were together, and there were idols there that had been offered to other Gods. You can still see where the images were and where a stream comes flowing out of the mountainside. It was a place of religious observance of other Gods. And Jesus looked at the disciples and said, 'Who do people say the Son of Man is?' They answered, 'Some say John the Baptist; others say Elijah; still others, Jeremiah or one of the prophets.' 'But what about you? Who do you say I am?' (Mt. 16.13–15).

Now, let's look at the witnessing of Jesus. He brought the question straight to them, kind of generally first, 'Who do people say the Son of Man is?' Many times as we share, we are sharing ideas of what someone said or what they've heard, but it all boils down to what do you think of Jesus. Who is He?

So when you witness, and when I witness, I try to explain who Christ is and let people understand and know the truth of the gospel; that He is God who came in the flesh without sin and lived and died and was resurrected. And as I proclaim the gospel message, then I always bring it to a final point, just like Jesus did. I say, 'What are you going to do with Jesus?' or, most of the time I put it this way, 'If you had the choice, and you do, of going with Jesus or without Him, which would you choose, the choice is yours? You can know Him now.' Jesus presented an invitation when He spoke, He always gave the opportunity to make that choice to follow Him, to trust Him, and so, as you witness I invite you to invite the people who you've talked with, to decide for Jesus Christ, to receive Him into their life as their Saviour.

DAY 11

I'm sure your witnessing is improving day by day as you look at Jesus Christ, sharing in every circumstance the message of salvation. Today let's look at Jesus in John chapter 11. As you study the chapter, you'll see a marvellous witness of Jesus, because here He brings salvation in the midst of death. You see him in every circumstance bringing life, now here is death.

A friend of Jesus, named Lazarus, died, leaving his two sisters, Mary and Martha. When

Lazarus had died, after great sickness, Jesus brought a great witness into the situation. You are faced with death and life, and friends of yours die, and friends of mine, and my father has died and so on. In the midst of death, we should deliver the good news. Let's see how Jesus does it.

Jesus said, 'and for your sake I am glad I was not there,' speaking of when Lazarus died, 'so that you may believe' (Jn. 11.15). In other words, if Jesus had been there, sure, He could have kept Lazarus whole, but he died. So, Jesus uses his death to cause people to believe.

Then they started questioning Jesus and Martha said, 'If you had been here, my brother would not have died' (Jn. 11.21). Listen to the words of Jesus, 'I am the resurrection and the life. He who believes in me will live, even though he dies; and whoever lives and believes in me will never die. Do you believe this?' (Jn. 11.25). Lazarus is already dead and buried and Jesus starts preaching. He was saying that if you believe in Him, you'll never die, your soul will live on. He was giving eternal life at that place of death when He said, 'I am the resurrection and the life.' Taking this circumstance of death and delivering a message of life.

And then Jesus went into the town and He called out for Lazarus to be resurrected, and Lazarus came out of the tomb, bound hand and foot, yes, but alive. I am always kind of amused to hear what Jesus said when He commanded, 'Lazarus, come out!' (Jn. 11.43). Have you ever wondered why Jesus said, 'Lazarus, come out'? I think it's because, if Jesus had just said 'Come out', every dead person in the world would have been resurrected. But He said, 'Lazarus, come out', eliminating the huge resurrection till later. And Lazarus came out, and notice what the Bible says next, 'Then many of the Jews who had come to visit Mary, and had seen what Jesus did, put their faith in Him' (Jn. 11.45). And listen to what Martha said, 'Yes, Lord, I believe that you are the Christ, the Son of God, who was to come into the world' (Jn. 11.27).

Jesus came into that place of death with Lazarus, brought him to life, worked a miracle and Martha said, 'You are the Christ', and all those who gathered around declared that He was the way, the truth and the life.

DAY 12

Today, I want to read John chapter 14. Jesus begins this witness to a group of people by saying, 'Do not let your hearts be troubled. Trust in God; trust also in me. In my Father's house are many rooms; if it were not so, I would have told you. I am going there to prepare a place for you' (Jn. 14.1, 2).

Jesus begins to witness by talking about heaven, by talking about what it's going to be like there, about His desire for us to be in heaven with Him. And as He shares this rich truth, Thomas says, 'Lord, we don't know where you are going, so how can we know the way?' (Jn. 14.5). So here is a person listening to Jesus talking about the joy of heaven, and asking about how we are going to get there. He wants to know the way and how to make it. And then Jesus said, 'I am the way and the truth and the life. No-one comes to the Father except through me' (Jn. 14.16). Here again we see the simplicity of the witness of Jesus Christ. Those listening wanted to go there and He told them how, in a straight, clear, pointed and unconfusing way, 'I. . .', He said, 'am the way, and the truth and the life.' What we are seeking for, He has it.

As you and I witness, we often take different approaches in our conversation with people. Sometimes you may just be talking about the great blessings of God, and people listen to you and say, 'Wow, you really are happy aren't you!' And you say, 'Yes, I am, and here's how you can be happy too. Give your life to Jesus Christ, receive Him as your Lord.' Jesus always communicated in a straightforward way and that should be our desire. With love, with compassion, and at various times, as you've seen through the days, you will see how Jesus adapted His message to the circumstances; how He spoke about something, and the people looked at Him and He told them how they could have it.

Often, people want the joy and assurance we have but we're very vague about it. So we need to explain who Jesus is – the Son of God who has come in the flesh, born to the virgin Mary, who rose again, is living, and will come again, and loves every one of us. I urge you to communicate the love of Jesus.

DAY 13

Today, let's look briefly at the life of Jesus and His witness on the Sermon on the Mount. Often we think of evangelists as great preachers standing up before a huge audience with microphones and wires everywhere, well, when Jesus preached His most famous sermon He was sitting down on a hillside. And that hillside was probably just grazing land for the sheep and the goats of the area. And He sat down and preached that mighty sermon. He made all those wonderful statements like 'Blessed are the poor in spirit; Blessed are those who mourn; Blessed are the meek; Blessed are those who hunger and thirst for righteousness; Blessed are the pure in heart,' and so on

(Mt. 5.3–8). He preached the most awesome sermon the world has ever heard. And if anybody knows anything about Jesus, they know about the Sermon on the Mount. It was so powerful and yet simple, so profound and yet so very readable.

This is what God wants us to do in our witness. Though we present a powerful message it should also be a message of simplicity; uncomplicated, simply sharing life and love and truth: there are two choices, with Him or without Him. There is life, and God loves us and He brought it together in a very powerful way.

When asked what is the great commandment, Jesus said, 'Love the Lord your God with all your heart and with all your soul, and with all your mind,' and 'Love your neighbour as yourself' (Mt. 23.37, 39). So, there was Jesus, sitting down, preaching the greatest sermon the world has ever known. Maybe you can sit down with somebody today and tell them how to be saved.

DAY 14

I'm going to look at Luke chapter 12 today, and as you read it you'll discover that some of the people who came to Jesus came with a problem. They asked him about a situation. One may say, 'Teacher, tell my brother to divide the inheritance with me' (Lk. 12.13). Now in our daily lives, people ask us various questions; we're faced with situations all the time, and so was Jesus. And what Jesus did was to take every situation that He found Himself in, every involvement with the affairs of others, and directly, He brought in the spiritual emphasis and declared the way of salvation. Isn't that the way you and I want to be a witness for Christ? Let's see what He did.

A man was asking Jesus to make his brother give him what was his. And Jesus said to him, 'Watch out! Be on your guard against all kinds of greed; a man's life does not consist in the abundance of his possessions' (Lk. 12.15). And then He told a parable about a rich man. Now what Jesus did was to give a truth; He said that life did not consist in the abundance of the things we possess.

There are times as we begin to live for the Lord when people ask a lot of questions. They say things like, 'Ah, the politicians are making a mess of the world', and you don't know what to say or do. But there you have a ripe opportunity to share with them and say, 'Well, you know the politicians, they make a mess but God has a plan for the world. One day Jesus is going to come again and even until He does, He can give us life, He can give us direction. We can live for Him'. See, we can use the questions people ask us.

Often people ask me which way to the airport or something, and I'll say, 'but more important than that, I can tell you how you can get to heaven. Jesus Christ saves and He loves you.' Sometimes I don't know the direction or the way to the airport because I'm a stranger in town, but I do know the way to heaven. Let's share that good news in the world.

DAY 15

I'm continuing to share with you the exciting life of Jesus Christ as He witnessed so that you and I may be more effective in sharing Christ with the world in which we live. So today I want to look at a very interesting and powerful aspect of Christ's life. It is Jesus, and the miracles He performed; His healing and His power over demonic spirits.

Listen to what the Scriptures say, 'the crowds were amazed at His teaching, because He taught as one who had authority, and not as their teachers of the law' (Mt. 7.28, 29). The Bible also says that Jesus healed all manner of sickness and disease among the lepers, among all the handicapped people, among the blind, and He raised the dead. He also had the power to multiply the loaves and the fishes.

Now what about Jesus and the miracles? Was He just working miracles as a sport? Did He do it all the time or was there a deeper meaning and purpose behind it? I find that as Jesus healed, the physical healing was not the ultimate, it was not, seemingly, His primary motivation. It was to teach another lesson; it was in order that people might know His authority.

Now until the time of Christ, there had been many prophets, there had been many mighty workers of God, and yet in Jesus we have one who comes and heals thousands of people. However, He did not heal everybody in all of Galilee and all of Judea and all of Samaria, but He did heal all the people that He wanted to heal. He healed all who requested healing of Him, but He did not just rapidly clear out every disease in the land.

Often Jesus was viewed only as a miracle worker. When Mary and Martha's brother, Lazarus, was sick, they sent for Jesus to come but He delayed and finally Lazarus died. And Martha said, 'Lord, if you had been here, my brother would not have died' (Jn. 11.21), but

Jesus had a greater motive, for after Lazarus died, Jesus raised him from the dead. This was to show his authority. It was to reveal Himself, and so He healed. He sent out His disciples to heal. And the early church healed in the name of Jesus. His healing powers are available today and He still heals the body. But it is realizing that the healing is to point to the manifestation that Jesus Christ is Lord, that He is Saviour. And that, through Him, people may have the greatest healing there is, and that is the inner healing of being forgiven of their sins; of being washed in the blood of Jesus. Spread that good news, and if you've never received Him, invite Jesus to be your Saviour today.

DAY 16

Let's look at how Jesus dealt with a man who was an antagonist, who was trying to criticize, and throw trick questions at Jesus. Often, as you witness, somebody will try trick questions. How did Jesus deal with it?

In Luke chapter 10, a man stood up and tried to justify himself, and tried to trick the Lord by asking, 'And who is my neighbour?' (Lk. 10.29).

Jesus was talking, and the man kept coming back with questions, so Jesus told the story of the Good Samaritan. He told how a man, (a Jew), was beaten and stripped and robbed, and when a priest came by and saw the man lying on the roadside, half dead, he went around him. Then another religious leader came by, saw the man and walked around him. Then a Samaritan came by who had a different ethnic and religious background (Samaritans were looked down on by Jews), and he saw this man beaten and lying almost dead on the roadside. And he went up to him and poured oil and wine on his wounds and bandaged him. He cared for him and took him to an inn. There he ministered to him and left money to take care of him, and arranged that if any more money was due, he'd pay for it when he returned.

Now let's look at this. Jesus then asked who the man's neighbour was. Was it the person who was of the same kindred ethnically, or a person who was of another background, even another religious viewpoint but who ministered to the needs of the brother? And the questioning man said, 'The one who had mercy on him,' and Jesus said, 'Go and do likewise' (Lk. 10.37).

I remember being driven down Sunset Strip in Hollywood one night, by a minister. As we went around some of the places where I often ministered, there was a drunk lying in the gutter. We both saw him and the minister began to preach, telling me how bad alcohol was, and we drove on. I said, 'Stop your car,' and I got out. I went back to the drunk man, picked him up, helped him across to the car and the minister said, 'No, he's going to mess my seat covers up. What am I going to do?' I said, 'I'll buy you new seat covers. I want to take this man down to our Halfway House and get him sober and saved.'

You see, we don't need to point our finger of judgement at this world. Our life must be involved in the world of ministering with the needs of person-to-person; not pointing a finger of condemnation, but an outstretched hand of love and mercy. As followers of Christ, our role is to share the good news, and love and help everybody.

DAY 17

Often when I've witnessed and shared Christ with someone, and they haven't received the Lord, it really hurts and I feel so bad. And we look at our witness and say that we want to witness better and yet we've failed. And if only we could witness like Billy Graham or Arthur Blessitt or someone like that, we'd be bringing people into the Kingdom of God all the time. However, when you look at Jesus, you need to realize that not everyone Jesus talked to received

Him as the Messiah. All of those whom Christ witnessed to received the truth, but not all of them received Him as Lord. So let's look at this part of the witnessing life of Christ.

In John chapter 6, we read how after Jesus had fed the 5,000, people went to Him the next day. They wanted more of the same kind of food; they wanted Him to do more for them. But Jesus said, 'I am the bread of life. He who comes to me will never go hungry, and he who believes in me will never be thirsty' (Jn. 6.60), but the people didn't want this kind of Jesus. And the Bible says, 'This is a hard teaching, who can accept it? (Jn. 6.60). And Jesus said, 'Does this offend you?' (Jn. 6.61). Then there are some tragic words, 'From this time many of His disciples turned back and no longer followed Him' (Jn. 6.66).

Jesus witnessed to these people, He explained the way of life: saying that He could satisfy the soul; that He could satisfy the thirst of life; that He could give value and meaning; that He loved them; that He was the object of life, and they wanted loaves and fishes. They didn't want the real Jesus, and so they left Him.

In Matthew chapter 19 we see the story of a young man who came to Jesus and said, 'Teacher, what good thing must I do to get eternal life?' and Jesus said, 'Obey the commandments.' And the man said, 'All these I have kept.' Jesus said, 'If you want to be perfect, go, sell your possessions and give to the poor, and you will have treasure in heaven. Then come, follow me.' And the Bible says 'he went away sad, because he had great wealth' (Mt. 19.16–22).

Jesus loved this man and spoke to him, and the young man met Christ and yet he left without becoming a follower of Jesus. Although it is a sad thing to say, and I must say it honestly, every person that I witness to does not receive Jesus. We should seek to present Christ, pray for people and encourage them in the Lord, and yet there is that knowledge some may never receive Jesus.

DAY 18

Today, I'm looking at Jesus as the critics viewed him. 'The Son of Man came eating and drinking . . . Here is a glutton and a drunkard, a friend of tax collectors and "sinners" ' (Lk. 7.35). Jesus was involved with sinners. He went where they were, they were his friends, He knew them and they knew Him.

One time a Pharisee invited Jesus to his house to eat with him, and the Scripture says, 'He went to the Pharisee's house and reclined at the table. When a woman who had lived a sinful life in that town learned that Jesus was eating at the Pharisee's house. . . .' (Lk. 7.36, 37). There are several interesting points here. One, Jesus was available. He was a friend and acquaintance of those who did not live righteous lives. He didn't just associate with the preachers, with those in the Temple, He was in contact with all of humanity. He went into an unsaved man's house and sat down in his home to eat dinner. When the other sinners around town heard that Jesus was in the house, they came, and one was a woman who was a sinner. And when she came in, she fell at the feet of Jesus and began to wash His feet with her tears, and as she wept and bathed His feet with her tears, the critics began to condemn Him, and said that He shouldn't do this; He shouldn't let this woman, who was a sinner, touch Him. And Jesus said, 'I came into your house. You did not give me any water for my feet, but she wet my feet with her tears and wiped them with her hair.' And He continued to speak, 'You did not put oil on my head, but she has poured perfume on my feet' (Lk. 7.44–46). As she washed His feet with the tears from her eyes, He showed how sinners, when their sins are forgiven, are greatly appreciative. He said to the woman, 'Your sins are forgiven,' and the guests said, 'Who is this who even forgives sins?', and Jesus said to the woman, 'Your faith has saved you; go in peace' (Lk. 7.48–50).

Jesus responded to the woman who loved Him. He didn't say that He was too holy, or that she couldn't be around Him, but He loved her, and He forgave her sins and He gave her a new life and she began to live victoriously and triumphantly. Jesus loves. You and I are to love. We are to identify ourselves with those who may not be Christians. You need them eating in your home and you need to be in their home. We need to go out into the streets, the highways and hedges, and compel people to come in to the house of God, that they may know Jesus. Praise God!

DAY 19

The book of Acts is a tremendous record of the early Christians reaching out into the world. We also want to be able to share Christ effectively and consistently and powerfully. We need knowledge, mixed with our zeal, and the enthusiasm of knowing Christ and living for Him today. So, for the next weeks I'm going to be looking at the book of Acts, to see how the early Christians shared the message. What empowered them? How were they able to mix in various backgrounds, with every obstacle against them, and find triumphant joy, and shake the world, literally, through their sharing of Christ?

Let's find one of the first problems the early Christians faced. In Acts chapter 1, when Jesus was about to ascend to the Father, He told His disciples that they were going to receive power, and that after the Holy Spirit had come upon them, they were to be witnesses in Jerusalem and Judea and Samaria and to the ends of the earth. Now, they wanted to know when He was coming again. But Jesus said, 'It is not for you to know the times or dates the Father has set by His own authority. But you will receive power when the Holy Spirit comes on you; and you will be my witnesses.' And then the Scripture says, 'He was taken up,' (Acts 1.7–9). And as He ascended into heaven the first thing the disciples did was to disobey what He had said. Because, instead of going into the city to proclaim and to preach and to prepare themselves, the Bible says, 'they were looking intently up into the sky as He was going,' and the Scripture says that two angels stood beside them and said, 'Why do you stand here looking into the sky? This same Jesus, who has been taken from you into heaven, will come back in the same way you have seen Him go into heaven' (Acts 1.10, 11).

Now, many of us believers are excited about Jesus coming again. Many of us want to know the day and the time. Everywhere I go, people ask about when Jesus is coming, and is now the time. And I say that 'I know now is the time to witness, and now is the time to proclaim the gospel of Jesus to everybody.' It was the commission of Jesus for us to go, and preach and be His witness.

God is looking at you today, and He is saying,

'Will you be my witness today?' He doesn't want you gazing at the ceiling, just gazing at the word, or just talking to Him, He wants you to talk to somebody about how they can be saved. You do that today and share Jesus Christ and His love with someone today.

DAY 20

Today I'm going to look in the Bible to see the mighty empowering of the Holy Spirit in the early believers' lives. You can find the story in Acts chapter 2. In the first verses, the Bible says, 'When the day of Pentecost came, they were all together in one place' (Acts 2.1). Here is one of the keys of the mighty effectiveness of these early believers – they were united; they were obsessed, and they were filled with the love of Jesus Christ. They knew in whom they believed. And then came the mighty anointing of the Holy Spirit; the mighty empowering of God's Spirit in their lives. Jesus had ascended into heaven and now the Spirit had come to reside within them.

When we receive Christ, we receive His Spirit and as we yield our life to Him, we receive the mighty empowering and filling of the baptism (the saturation) of the Holy Spirit. To do what? To feel good? It's wonderful to be filled with the Spirit, to be happy, but to do what?

Notice what happened when the early believers were filled. The Bible says, 'staying in Jerusalem were God-fearing Jews from every nation under heaven' (Acts 2.5). Now, these early believers, filled with the Holy Spirit, confounded the multitude who had come together because they heard them speak in their own language. What joy it is to know that God wants to communicate His message in a way that people can understand it. And they understood about the Lord.

What did those witnesses talk about on the day of Pentecost? – the wonderful works of God. What is the wonderful work of God? – it is His love, poured out; that while we were yet sinners, Christ died for us. The wonderful work of God is that His Spirit is here to convict us of sin, to bring us to repentance and into a newness of life – that is the life Jesus wants you to have. It is to be filled with His Spirit, empowered by Him, to speak His wonderful works. How are people going to hear without a preacher? How are they going to know these wonderful works unless you tell them?

DAY 21

The Bible tells us in Acts chapter 2, that when the disciples were filled with the Holy Spirit on the day of Pentecost, the people thought that they were drunk. But Peter told them how they were filled with the Spirit, according to the prophet Joel. Then Peter began to preach a message that every Christian needs to use in their witnessing. He starts off with what he and others had been accused of, (being drunk), and then shared with them how they too could know the Lord. He preached Christ and Christ crucified. He said that God had already provided their salvation; that God loved them; that Jesus died upon the cross; that He'd been resurrected from the dead and that this Jesus was alive, and he knew it because he had seen the crucifixion and he had seen the resurrected Christ. And then he said that they needed to receive Him as Lord and Christ. Then, listen to these words, 'When the people heard this, they were cut to the heart,' and they asked Peter what they must do. And Peter said, 'Repent and be baptized, every one of you, in the name of Jesus Christ' (Acts 2. 37, 38).

As I studied the witnessing life of Jesus, when He began to preach, He preached repentance for the Kingdom of heaven is at hand (Mt. 3.2). John the Baptist was also preaching repentance.

And now, the day after Pentecost, what were they doing? – they started off preaching 'Repent'. So, for us today, when we share the good news of Jesus Christ, in joy, in happiness, in excitement, in love, and it may seem unusual to you, but it's natural to be happy and to live an abundant life as a Christian; we must also point out that people need to repent of their sins and turn from the life that is destined to separate them from God in hell, and to give themselves to Jesus. And when you share the gospel, as Peter shared the gospel, people will come under repentance, and there will be that inward desire to know Jesus and be saved.

DAY 22

Let's look at the mark of a real evangelist for Jesus Christ. Peter has been preaching on the day of Pentecost, crowds have gathered in the streets and he's proclaimed the good news of Jesus Christ; the death of Christ and the resurrection, and the fact that they need to repent and to receive Him as their Lord. And then, listen to this evangelist give his invitation. 'With many other words he warned them; and he pleaded with them, "save yourselves from this corrupt generation" ' (Acts 2.40). This is the real mark of an evangelist, isn't it? With many words he preached, explained, encouraged and said, 'Save yourself.'

For believers who are going to witness for Christ, it is vitally important to bring the invitation home to the person, to be able to say to them, 'Repent, receive Jesus now.' If your heart doesn't burn, desiring the conversion of the lost, then you're not going to see great results. But in Peter we see that evangelistic heart saying, 'Save yourselves.'

And what happened? The Bible says, 'Those who accepted his message were baptized, and about three thousand were added to their number that day' (Acts 2.41). This is how the early church started with the message of Christ; with the flaming heart of an evangelist, and the people gladly receiving Him. And the Scriptures say, 'They devoted themselves to the apostles' teaching and fellowship, to the breaking of bread and to prayer' (Acts 2.42). The apostles answered their questions, led them to Jesus and then they helped them to study the Bible, to know the truth. This is the way that we as Christ's followers today should live our lives. In the power of the Holy Spirit and in urging the unsaved to trust Jesus.

I encourage you today, if you have a friend or neighbour, or someone you've been witnessing to, and they've never received Christ, invite them to Jesus. Some people don't encourage pushing, but I'd rather push somebody toward heaven than just let them slide into hell. Encourage somebody today to receive Jesus Christ.

DAY 23

I'm continuing to study the witnessing life of the early believers in the book of Acts, to see how they lived, how they witnessed and what they talked about. In chapter 3, Peter and John entered the temple, and as they went in, a lame man was lying there – sick and infirm from his mother's womb – and he was begging for alms. Peter and John walked by and said, 'Look at us!' and the guy looked up at them and they said, 'Silver or gold I do not have but what I have I give you. In the name of Jesus Christ of Nazareth, walk' (Acts 3.1–6). These are powerful words and they mean much to us today. They had no silver or gold; they didn't have anything to give that was physical; they were broke, but they had Jesus Christ and He can put a man's life together, forever.

And so I'm going to ask you, what do you have? They said they had no silver or gold, but they had Jesus Christ. And God wants to use you and everything you have for His glory. You may have some religious magazines or gospel materials which you've already read and would normally throw out in the rubbish. Don't do that any more. Take them down to the launderette, and leave the gospel material on the table where the magazines are. When you go to the dentist or doctor, or wherever you go, leave one of those gospel materials. Some of you have many Bibles, leave them around. What do you have? You have letters that you send to friends, insert a gospel tract in those envelopes and post them. When you pay your bills, slip in a gospel tract or a Jesus sticker.

Do you have a friend you can share with? Maybe invite them over for lunch, or meet them for their lunch at work. When talking about different things, you can share with them about Jesus Christ. You can ask them simply, 'Do you know Jesus Christ as your Saviour?' Or it may be that they're sharing some need in their life and you can say, 'Oh, let me show you how that need can be met'. And you might read them, 'My God will meet all your needs according to His glorious riches in Christ Jesus' (Phil. 4.19). Communicate with somebody about the Lord today.

DAY 24

We've just seen how Peter and John saw the lame man healed. How he came leaping up, praising God and the crowds gathered round. They knew this man had been lame, they had seen him begging for years, and now he was whole and praising God. And they started questioning Peter and John about his healing. And Peter and John began to witness to the crowd. They took advantage of the interest of the people, to communicate the message of Jesus Christ. Now, often that is what we need to do. Maybe you've just bought a new car and people are looking at that car – 'Oh, what a wonderful car you've got,' and you'll say, 'Yes, this is a mighty fine car, but you know what, it cost me a lot of money and it's going to wear out. But that's not true about Jesus Christ, because the greatest thing in the world was free, Jesus died for me and my relationship with Him will never die.' Just take something and change it.

Peter and John could have started a debate on the miracle, but what did they do? They said, 'Repent then, and turn to God, so that your sins may be wiped out' (Acts 2.19). They proclaimed the redemptive message. Now when you witness, it is very important to learn from these early believers. When they witnessed they preached Christ, they shared Jesus Christ.

Often, when you start witnessing you find yourself led into a conversation or a debate, or you find yourself talking about politics or the weather, or talking about ball games, and you just can't seem to stick to the subject. Talk about Jesus; people want to talk about Him; they want to know about their relationship with God. Sometimes they might not be interested in church but they are interested in their lives being filled with life and love and joy. They're interested in their relationship with God, so talk about Jesus. Show them how He will meet their needs and then bring them, once they have given their lives to Jesus Christ, to understand what the Church is and how they can study the Bible and grow. But don't get hung up on the side issues, concentrate on the main thing and that is our Lord.

DAY 25

In Acts chapter 4 I see something marvellous about a man who only a few weeks earlier had denied that he even knew Jesus Christ. It was Peter, and Peter had denied that he knew Jesus just before the crucifixion. He quit following

Christ and became a fisherman again, and Jesus went back and got him, and he was filled with the Holy Spirit and then he preached on the day of Pentecost. Listen to the words in Acts, 'When they saw the courage of Peter and John and realized that they were unschooled, ordinary men, they were astonished and they took note that these men had been with Jesus' (Acts 4.13). Peter and John did not come from the intellectual circles of Jerusalem, their background was fishing and manual labour. Peter was a thick-headed muscle man type, but he was full of the anointing of God. And God transformed him and made him a bold and dynamic witness for Jesus Christ. That is what God wants to do for you.

'For God did not give us a spirit of timidity, but a spirit of power, of love and of self-discipline' (2 Tim. 1.7). Listen to what the spirit-filled Peter and John said when hauled before the authorities in Acts, 'Judge for yourselves whether it is right in God's sight to obey you rather than God. For we cannot help speaking about what we have seen and heard' (Acts 4.19, 20). This is marvellous! They had been commanded not to preach or teach in the name of Jesus Christ, and here they were again, commanded by the authorities to cease preaching, and what was their reaction? Their reaction was that they were so full on the inside that although a law had just been passed outlawing preaching, they couldn't help but speak those things which they had seen and heard.

Many times, as I minister around the world,

I find in my encounters with believers, many of them give excuses about their lack of witness. And sometimes I've tried to crank them up, or I've tried to prime the pump, so to speak, and get them going for the Lord.

I grew up on a farm in Louisiana and discovered that when we used the pump on the farm, we had to pour a little water in the pump top, priming the pump. And you'd pump, and finally it'd catch the water, 30 or 40 feet below, and the pump would prime, and out would come the water. Now, you had to keep priming the pump, and it wasn't sealed good, and it wasn't in good shape. I think a lot of believers are like that. As a matter of fact, some believers have never even got plugged into the well, and you pump and you pump and you try to get the water to come out and no water ever comes out.

You need to be so full of Jesus that you can't help witnessing, you'll want to, it's not a job that you have to do, it's not a command that you must obey. It is a relationship with Jesus that you can't shut up about, that you can't stop speaking about. It is Jesus and you're excited. It's like being in love. Be in love with Jesus, and go out today and share the love and message of Jesus with somebody.

DAY 26

I continue to study the life of the early witnesses in Acts chapters 4 and 5, who were threatened with being beaten, stoned and killed. But they said they couldn't help but speak those things which they had seen and heard. And when they were assembled together, 'They were all filled with the Holy Spirit and spoke the Word of God boldly' and 'All the believers were one in heart and mind. No-one claimed that any of his possessions was his own, but they shared everything they had. With great power the apostles continued to testify to the resurrection of the Lord Jesus' (Acts 4.31–33). Isn't that wonderful! God blessed that church with great power, and the place was shaken. And when they went out, after being commanded not to preach and not to teach, they were beaten again, and the Scripture says, 'left . . . rejoicing because they had been counted worthy of suffering disgrace for the Name,' and 'Day after day, in the temple courts and from house to house, they never stopped teaching and proclaiming the good news that Jesus is the Christ' (Acts 5.41, 42).

The commission was given to us as individuals, and to the Church, to go out and communicate Jesus Christ. Where did the early Christians go? They met together in the temple. They met together as a church and there received strength, knowledge, power and filling. And then, what did they do? They went into the neighbourhood, house to house.

Do you say you're a part of a real Bible church? Then are you going house to house, teaching in the name of Jesus? You need to go to your next-door neighbour, on either side of your house. Knock on their door, tell them who you are, introduce yourself and say, 'I'm interested in your relationship with God. I love you. If you die now, where would you spend eternity?' And say, 'I brought along a little Bible, I'd like to give to you.' Start evangelizing in your neighbourhood. Get your church together and systematically visit every house in the neighbourhood. Get out there and go for God!

DAY 27

Today I'm looking at how different people in the early days communicated the message of Jesus Christ, and in Acts chapters 6 and 7, I'm studying a man called Stephen. He was not a preacher per se; he was a layman. Notice what was said about Stephen, 'but they could not stand up against his wisdom or the Spirit by which he spoke' (Acts 6.10). What a wonderful thing to be said about a person's witness for Jesus Christ. The man was full of wisdom and mightily filled with the Holy Spirit of God.

The Bible says that we should study to show ourselves approved by God. We've got to grow in Christ, we must study and pray; and to have true wisdom is a mighty virtue. And the Bible says this is what characterizes Stephen's life. At the end of his life, he was taken to trial, and notice what was said, 'The Sanhedrin looked intently at Stephen, and they saw that his face was like the face of an angel' (Acts 6.15). What a man of God! What a witness! Even to look at him it seemed that there was the glow of the angel. And yet, as Stephen witnessed, the people did not receive Christ as their Saviour. What happened? The Bible tells us that they became angry at his sermon and began to threaten him and finally they pounced on him and began to beat him, and even to bite him with their teeth. And the Scriptures says, 'he saw the glory of God, and Jesus standing at the right hand of God' (Acts 7.55). Then they took him out of the city and stoned him to death. But before he died he cried out, 'Lord do not hold this sin against them. When he had said this, he fell asleep' (Acts 7.60).

Stephen was a mighty witness and an example that you and I should seek to emulate in our living. Full of wisdom, full of the Spirit and yet even though he witnessed effectively, the people did not receive his message. Sometimes people will reject you, as they rejected Stephen, and yet even at his death, people were converted. Stephen died, full of love, bearing no resentment or hatred for all the ridicule and persecution received, but praising God and rejoicing that he was counted worthy to suffer for Jesus Christ.

DAY 28

For the next few days I'm going to look at a story in the Bible that is really powerful and full of life, and I think that it's going to help you evaluate yourself and make a difference in your witnessing life. It's in Acts chapter 8 and it's the story about Philip who went out, led by the Spirit to an Ethiopian eunuch.

'Now an angel of the Lord said to Philip, "Go south to the road – the desert road – that goes down from Jerusalem to Gaza". So he started out' (Acts 8.26, 27). The Lord had shown Philip that he had something for him to do. He had to leave where he was, to get to the road that went from Jerusalem to Gaza, and immediately Philip obeyed the Lord. He got up and he went.

Many of you have been saying that God's been speaking to us in our lives and yet we haven't got up and gone. We never get started, and the Lord wants us to go. The Lord didn't describe every detail to Philip, He just wanted him to go there, and He would lead the way. That is what God has promised us. Jesus has said that He will be with us, until the end of the world. When the Lord is with you don't fear, but go.

For some of you, God has called you to preach, but you have never surrendered. It's time now to arise and go and do what God told you to do. For some of you God has wanted you on the mission field, and you've given excuse after excuse after excuse. Don't give Him your excuse, give Him your life. If God says go to New York, you'd better get to New York any way; if you've got the money fly there; if you don't have the money, drive there in your car. If your car won't make it and you don't have the money for the petrol, hitchhike and you'll make it. If nobody will pick you up, then get out there and walk – you can make it. I walked across America in six months. If you can't walk, then crawl, and if you can't crawl then fall in that direction, and God will bless you. The Lord said to Philip 'Go' and Philip got up and went.

DAY 29

Philip obeyed. He went down to the road between Jerusalem and Gaza, the Spirit having led him there, and that's all the Lord had told him to do. He went there and stood on the roadside, right out in the middle of the desert. There he stood and all of a sudden, along came a chariot pulled by horses; and there was a man in the chariot, and he had all sorts of goods and servants. There he was, and suddenly the Spirit said to Philip, 'Go to that chariot and stay near it' (Acts 8.29). Probably there was a whole caravan, because it seems that this man was rich. He had been tending to business and there were probably several chariots, camels and all kinds of things. The caravan was passing by, and the Lord pointed out to Philip to go over and join that one chariot.

Here was Philip and the chariots going by, and the Lord showed him which one it was, and Philip ran forward. He ran beside the horses; and the man was reading an Old Testament scroll aloud. He was reading the Word of God but he didn't understand what he was reading. (You'd better be in shape if you're going to witness for the Lord, He might have you running alongside of some Jaguar some day!) And Philip said, 'Do you understand what you are reading?', and the man said, 'How can I unless someone explains it to me?' (Acts 8.30–31). And the man invited him up.

We know that the chariot was still on the move because later on, when the man got ready for his baptism, he demanded the chariot to stop. Now some of you think that that's strange, and yes, it is. But the Lord uses strange things for His glory. It was God's way, and there may be some unusual things in witnessing that God wants you to do. But don't worry about the critics, be concerned about the message and get out there and obey the Spirit.

DAY 30

In Acts chapter 8, after Philip had got alongside the chariot, he asked the man, 'Do you understand what you are reading?' (Acts 8.30). There was this Ethiopian eunuch; a man in charge of all the treasure of the Queen in Ethiopia; a man of great authority; an intellectual; a man of knowledge; a man of business and commerce; an educated person, and Philip asked him if he knew what he was reading. And the man said, 'How can I, unless someone explains it to me?' (Acts 8.31).

How can a person know Jesus unless somebody guides them. This is so essential for us as witnesses to understand. People need the gospel message explained. Many people do not understand about the Lord. Many scientists know how to get a man on the moon, but they don't know how to get their life together. They now know how to work or build computers, but they don't know how to relate to their wife, or their children, or to their next-door neighbour. How will a person know how to be saved? The Bible says that someone needs to tell them.

So Philip sat in the chariot with this man and began to speak. 'Then Philip began with that very passage of Scripture and told him the good news about Jesus' (Acts 8.35). This is what the world needs, Jesus. This man might have been able to run circles around Philip if they'd been discussing finance; he might have been able to run circles around Philip if they'd been discussing world geography, because Philip hadn't travelled much. But when they started talking about spiritual things, Philip was the expert and this man was the one that needed to be taught. And the Scripture says that he taught him about Jesus, beginning with the Scripture that he was reading. As he taught, he used the word of God.

As you witness, I would encourage you to use the word of God. I like to show a person the Scriptures; the word of God, so that they understand and know that what I'm saying is from the Bible. We need to concentrate on Jesus Christ. There are many people who don't understand the miracles; or how Jesus walked on the water, for example. But when you show them who He is; that He is God who came in the flesh. When you teach about Jesus, you can see when people know Jesus, because they understand that He has all the power in His hands; that He has the authority and the power to meet every need. Share Jesus with somebody today and spread the love of Christ all around the world.

DAY 31

I'm still looking at the life of Philip today, and seeing a beautiful story of how he witnessed. Philip preached to this intellectual man about Jesus and the man wanted to be baptized, and Philip said, 'If you believe with all your heart, you may.' And he answered, 'I believe that Jesus Christ is the Son of God' (Acts 8.37). Philip had done a good job.

Many of us have witnessed to people, but we haven't really explained the gospel. Often we just drop little titbits about Jesus and say that we trust they'll come to church with us sometime. But, you need to zero right in and say, 'I've been talking to you about Jesus, and right now, I want to ask you to pray, and I'll lead you in prayer, that you may receive Jesus as your Saviour.' You need to invite that person to receive Christ. Many of us have talked about Jesus, but never invited the person to make a decision.

The man said, 'I believe,' and so they stopped the chariot where there was some water and Philip baptized him. Maybe it was some kind of an oasis, or whatever it was, Philip got down there and baptized him. Now look what happened. They went down into the water and when they came up out of the water the Spirit of the Lord caught up Philip and the eunuch never saw him again, and he went on his way rejoicing.

What about the follow-up? On the day of Pentecost we find that the new believers immediately joined the disciples and continued steadfastly in the apostles' doctrine and fellowship. They got day by day nurture in fellowship. But here we find that immediately after the Ethiopian had been saved, and baptized, Philip was jerked away. Some people say that if you can't really follow-up the person, then it's a waste of time to lead him to Jesus. What happened here? It wasn't Philip who decided to leave – the Spirit took him away. Sometimes, when you pray with a person who lives in another state or another country and there's no way to get in touch, you go ahead and pray with them, and lead them to Jesus. If the Lord has brought you to them, that they might be saved, then God will strengthen them or bring somebody else to them so that they'll be strengthened in the gospel. But lead people to Christ.

DAY 32

As I've been looking at the witnessing life of the believers, one thing I noticed is in Acts chapter 13. As they spoke and witnessed, they ran into some opposition, but notice these words, 'When the proconsul saw what had happened, he believed, for he was amazed at the teaching about the Lord' (Acts 13.12). Here we see a man who was converted, not only because of what Paul said but also because of what he saw God doing and how he saw them living.

Every one of us needs to be speaking the message of Jesus with our lips, but we also need to live a life that is radiant; transmitting the real beauty of God. A person looking into your face needs to see the radiance of Jesus, and when they see the way you love, the way you are, the way you are sincerely interested in helping others, then they say that they believe there really is something to that because they see the way the person is living. Another thing we see is that their lives were full of hazards for the name of the Lord Jesus Christ. They were willing to jeopardize their lives and yet they were full of joy and full of victory.

In chapter 14 I note one very important thing. Paul and the apostles had been witnessing and sharing about the Lord Jesus Christ, in the city of Lystra, and we find that Paul was beaten and stoned, 'They stoned Paul and dragged him outside the city, thinking he was dead. But after the disciples had gathered round him, he got up and went back into the city. The next day he and Barnabas left for Derbe' (Acts 14.19, 20). And the Bible says in the next verse, 'they preached the good news in that city and won a large number of disciples. Then they returned to Lystra' (Acts 14.21). Paul was stoned until his attackers thought he was dead, and then thrown out of Lystra, as a dead man. He must have been battered and beaten and bloody when lying outside the city, and yet the Bible says that he went back to the very same city and he preached.

People are still suffering and dying for Jesus, God has blessed us! Let us be full of His joy, and discover the privilege it is to hazard our life for the glory of God.

DAY 33

The early disciples of Jesus always brought their message to a point of decision; they didn't just speak the word of God and witness. And in Acts chapter 26 we see Paul brought before King Agrippa. Listen to these words. 'King Agrippa, do you believe the prophets? I know you do.' Then Agrippa said to Paul, 'Do you think that in such a short time you can persuade me to be a Christian?' Paul replied 'Short time or long – I pray God that not only you but all who are listening to me today may become what I am, except for these chains' (which meant that he was a captive in jail) (Acts 26.27–29). Paul was saying that he didn't want the King to be almost, but altogether persuaded that Jesus Christ is the Son of God. I urge you to look at these words in the Bible and note that as he witnessed, he brought his witness to a point of decision.

The early Christians also had a sensitivity to the people they talked to. When Paul was brought before king after king and trial after trial, when he was completely guiltless, and had no crime against him, and no reason to be there, he didn't look at the judge or the king and say, 'You dirty scoundrel, you ought to be in jail yourself for putting me in jail.' You don't see any bitterness. Instead Paul says, 'I consider myself fortunate to stand before you today as I make my defence. . . ' and 'especially so because you are well acquainted with all the Jewish customs and controversies' (Acts 26.2, 3). Paul is kind of building up the guy's ego. He's saying that he knows he's an expert in the field, so he can be sure of a fair trial. He honours the king, he says, 'King Agrippa' and he talks on and on to King Agrippa, and just as when he met Governor Felix, he speaks with kindness. Even when Paul preached on Mars Hill in Athens, proclaiming the Word about the unknown God, he started off at the people's point of interest. He didn't bitterly attack them, he shared and communicated.

We need to share the message of Jesus in Love, and beauty. That doesn't mean that we're wishy-washy and weak, or that we don't have a powerful message of witness. It's that person to person and individual to individual contact. We don't just bulldozer over people, but we share with them what they need in their life. Sometimes Christians start screaming; getting loud in witnessing, and fussing. Loud voices don't save anybody, it's the Holy Spirit. Love the people, and share in gentleness and in love the message of Jesus Christ today.

DAY 34

What I'm going to study now is difficult questions, and things people say as we share Christ with them. Many times a person will almost blow us away with, 'I don't believe in God,' or 'I'm an atheist,' and we don't know what to say. When somebody says that to me, I simply smile real big and say they're smarter than that. I look at them, and say that they've got reasonable sense, that they know there's a God. All of us know there's a God. See, there are some people who say that they're atheists just to shake you up and keep you from talking to them about the Lord. So I respond in that way and then say, 'The Bible says . . .', and just go right into the way of salvation.

There are other people who have sincerely deep doubts and questions as to whether there is a God or not, and so to that person we should share an answer. The Bible says, 'The fool says in his heart, "There is no God" ' (Ps. 14.1). So a person who doesn't believe in God is foolish in their mind. But perhaps when we enlighten people, to help them see, they then understand and receive the Lord.

I've led many people to Jesus who have said they're atheists. Sometimes I'll use an illustration, and say, 'Look at this watch,' and I'll point to it and say, 'Did this watch just happen or was it made? They'll say, 'Why, of course it was made,' and I'll say, 'You see, a watch is a reflection of mind, creativity and power. A person had to think of a watch and envisage it in his mind. A person then had to have creativity in order to make the moulds and the power – the power to do it.' I say, 'This is like a reflection of the way God is. We look at the world around us and we see this – we look at our body and our body is far more complicated than a watch. So how can you deny that our God didn't make us or that God has nothing to do with this? No, the very evidence of the universe declares the handiwork of God.'

Sometimes I'll say, 'It's wonderful to be able to talk to you and to share with you. We can feel love and emotions, and we can have love for our wife and children and the world. We are made in order to have all these emotions, and the intricate mind and feelings that we have; made by a God who also has feelings, who can communicate; we're made in His image and He wants you to know Him. You can know human love. You can talk with man but the ultimate is to know the love of God, to communicate with the Creator, and He's interested in you and you can invite Him into your life. He has rebuilt Himself in Jesus Christ the Saviour. Receive Him.' So don't turn off when you speak to an atheist, turn him on to Jesus Christ.

DAY 35

As we begin to witness, some people come right back and say, 'But I'm too far gone – there's just no way that God can save me.' Over and over I talk with people on skid row, I talk with people who are affluent, and millionaires, and yet in their mind, they've done everything, they've been everywhere and they say, 'But life's not worth living – I'm too far gone, there's nothing that can be done for me'. But listen to what the Bible says, 'Surely the arm of the Lord is not too short to save, nor his ear too dull to hear' (Isa. 59.1). If you haven't sought the love and the outreaching arms of Jesus Christ, then it is this message that we as believers have the joy of sharing everywhere we go. People are not too far gone.

Look in the Bible where God took Moses, who really was a murderer, and used him to be the mighty leader of the children of Israel. God chose another man in the New Testament, who was persecuting the Christians and who consented to the murder and stoning of Stephen, and God called Saul and changed his name to Paul and he became a mighty leader of the early Church and wrote many of the books in the Bible. God delights in putting broken lives back together again.

Many of us look at ourselves in such despair

but the evangelist, the witness, the Christian, is to communicate the message, 'No, you're not too far gone, God is right where you are.' Jesus said, 'I stand at the door and knock. If anyone hears my voice, and opens the door, I will go in and eat with him, and he with me' (Rev. 3.20). So when somebody tells you they are too far gone, don't let that restrain you, share with them, that whoever calls on the name of the Lord, shall be saved. Whoever – that's God calling. Whoever – it doesn't matter what you've done, how you've lived; you communicate with them the good news. It's been one of the great joys in my life, to be able to go into the streets and bars and to all kinds of troubled people, and to declare to them that there is good news, there is hope. So I challenge you Christians, let's go into this troubled world and let them know, people can be saved.

DAY 36

Have you ever met anybody who's really good? I mean, they're so good they tell you that they're good enough, and that they don't need the Lord. A lot of times when we're sharing Jesus, somebody seems to sit there in their perfection and we don't know what to say. We know how to talk to a person who's really sinned a lot, but if a person happens to say, 'I'm in good shape, I don't need the Lord,' what do you say then? Well, there are many Scripture verses that you could use, but I find that one of my favourites is in Jeremiah, 'The heart is deceitful above all things and beyond cure. Who can understand it?' (Jer. 17.9). If somebody says that they don't need God, they're in good shape, and everything is together, I say, 'but God says that the heart is desperately wicked.' Every one of us has sinned.

Sin is coming short of the glory of God; sin is turning from God to ourself, and every person has sinned against God. There is nobody who has ever perfectly lived up to their own standard. There is nobody who has perfectly lived up to society's standard. And there is nobody, especially, who has lived up to God's standard. And I have never had anybody say, 'I'm as good as Jesus, I have worked the miracles that Jesus has worked, I have loved the way Jesus loved.' We recognize that it is not our goodness that saves us, but it is the grace of God. Having come short of the grace of God; having come short of absolute and total perfection, we're sinners. In my witness, most of the time, I find people will acknowledge their sin but sometimes I run across a person who says that they don't need Him, they're in good shape. In that situation, just come right back to the Scriptures; don't condemn, don't judge, just point out if they have ever in all their life done one thing that was less than perfect, and they'll say, 'Certainly,'; you say, 'then we all need Jesus'.

Or I might say, 'You didn't make yourself did you?' and they'll say, 'Oh, well, my mom and dad did,' and I'll say, 'but they didn't really know all the mechanics of how it works'. You see, we don't understand all about creation, about how that which is not becomes that which is now – because God created it. God makes us and we're responsible to God and we do need Him. We need Him because He is the one that made us, He is the one that keeps us alive. Many people say that they don't believe in God and don't want anything to do with Him. And people even curse Him; the atheist curses God with the breath that God gives, and with the strength that God gives him. If God removed His hand we would not even be dust, we would be nothing, not even one cell, not even one atom. And He is also the one who judges.

He does love us, and He does care for us. We need Him to give us the right perspective of life, we need Him to forgive us our sins. We need Him to make heaven our home. We need Him to put His spirit in us and fill us with His life, which is the greatest blessing in the world.

DAY 37

Have you ever shared Jesus Christ with someone who was really interested when you told them about the Lord and the love of Jesus Christ, and then you've asked that person to receive Jesus as their Saviour, and they have said to you, 'Oh, I don't think that I need to receive him as my Saviour, but I love who Jesus was. He was a good man, and He said good things and He is my example'.

One of the most prominent politicians in America, who was a Presidential candidate, said to me, 'Jesus is my example, He is my standard of living, but I do not believe that He was resurrected. I don't believe that He worked the miracles that He worked. He was a good man, the best man the world has ever seen, and He lives through His ideas, as we live His ideas.' But what if somebody says that to you? I always like to look back to the Scriptures and point out that Jesus Christ was not just a good man. He was either who He said He was, or He was the greatest deceiver and liar of all times. He was either the greatest fraud that ever walked this earth or He is Lord of all. He claimed to have the power to forgive sin; we see Him working miracles; have Him teaching about hell; have Him claiming that He was God; that He was going to be crucified and resurrected; that He was coming again. Anybody who would lie that much is not a good man. So, He was either a liar, deceived by His own self, or Jesus Christ, the Son of God.

Now we know that He is the Son of God. How do we know that He's not like every other man and just a good man? Because He was born of the virgin Mary, because He was conceived not by the seed of man, but by the Holy Spirit. Isn't that beautiful? He was conceived in the womb by the breathing of the Holy Spirit. Jesus lived without sin, never at fault in His whole life. Then again, Jesus worked mighty miracles that were seen by thousands and thousands of people. It was true, they saw His miracles. The critics of Jesus never accused Him of not working miracles. Those who tried to accuse Him of something, tried to say that He was doing it in the power of the devil, but they couldn't refute His mighty miracles.

Jesus was unique in His resurrection, but not in His death. Sure, He was unique in that He bore our sins, but I mean from a worldly standard. Everybody dies, but Jesus was resurrected. He is alive. He ascended into heaven. Jesus Christ fulfils the Scriptures. We know that Jesus is not just a good man, we know that He is the man of history. He is the truth, the Bible declares that, and you can share with a person that they can receive Him into their life and know this Jesus as Lord, as a friend, as their closest companion. So, share with your friends about Jesus, and any of you that need to know Him and have never received Him, I invite you to ask Jesus into your life.

DAY 38

As I travel around and see the beauty of the world, I see the reflection of God, but often as I witness, and as you witness, we come across people who say, 'Well, nature is my God, just nature. All I need is to get out for a weekend and I feel better, that's all I need. That's my God, nature'.

Many Christians don't know how to witness to people who seem to be sensitive to nature. What I see in a person really wrapped up in nature, is that they are responding to the reflection of God, but they need to know Him. Nature cannot save you. Birds and flowers and fish cannot wash away your sins, but Jesus can. Just listen to what the Bible says, 'Now this is eternal life; that they may know you, the only true God, and Jesus Christ, whom you have sent' (Jn. 17.3). It's necessary to know more than nature. Go from nature to the creator and point the way. The Bible says, 'The heavens declare the glory of God' (Ps. 19.1), and all the works that God made in this world reflect and show Him. So, we must come from the beauty of creation to the creator.

It is necessary to know the only true God, the God who made nature. And if you find joy and delight and beauty in nature, how much more thrilled you're going to be with the God who created that nature. And so when I witness, I point that out. I don't condemn people for loving nature, but I point out that as they experience this beauty, there is so much more that they can know, because although nature has its beauty, when we look at ourselves, and we're a creation of God, we see our sin. So we're not as pure. The Bible says over and over in Romans, 'The creation waits in eager expectation for the sons of God to be revealed', and 'We know that the whole creation has been groaning. . .' (Rom. 8.19, 22). And we so long for that peace, and Jesus Christ gives that peace. So if you love nature, look beyond nature and realize that God has manifested Himself in Jesus and that when we know Jesus, we know the creator of all, because the Bible says, 'without Him nothing was made that has been made' (Jn. 1.3). So you can know the God who created this world.

DAY 39

Sometimes people will ask questions or give answers that really sidetrack you. So, this is what I'm dealing with now; how to answer a person who comes up with something that you don't know how to deal with. Some people say, 'I'd like to be a Christian, but it just seems so confusing to me. I'm confused about religion'. Maybe it's because my mind is so simple, but I have a happy relationship in my fellowship with God, because to me Christianity is very simple. It's not confusing, it's not complex, the Bible is very simple. It's a message from God to let you know He loves you. It's a message from God to show us what's gone wrong. It's a message from God to tell us how it can be put right. It is God's message of redemption that can deliver us from the turmoil we're in.

Listen to this, and I believe you'll be able to understand it, and use it when you witness. A lawyer was talking to Jesus and asked him, 'Teacher, which is the greatest commandment in the Law?' (Mt. 22.36). They had thousands of laws that they had to keep and it was very confusing. This man was saying, 'Which one should I keep? I can't keep them all, what do I do?' And listen to what Jesus said, 'Love the Lord your God with all your heart and with all your soul, and with all your mind. This is the first and greatest commandment' (Mt. 22.37,38). Now is that confusing? 'Love the Lord your God with all your heart' – that's not confusing. It may be more difficult to do, it may take everything you've got, to do, but that's what it's all about – loving the Lord. And the second is like it, 'Love your neighbour as yourself. All the Law and the Prophets hang on these two commandments' (Mt. 22.40).

So Christianity is very simple. Jesus Christ is the very centre of our faith. Without Jesus, there is no Christianity. Christianity is not rules and regulations and laws, it is a relationship with the person, Jesus Christ, who came in the flesh, lived, died, rose again and is ascended into the Father. And you can receive Him into your life and know Him, and that is the message the Christian is to share. It's not confusing.

Now if you start talking about all the functions of your church and how you vote on all the procedures and all the doctrines and all the intricacies of the second coming, or all the different viewpoints of the millennium reign of Jesus, or the Judgement; people can get confused. The message is love Him with all your heart, and love your neighbour as yourself. Very simple, very powerful and totally the truth. So point people to Christ, invite people to know Jesus.

DAY 40

As I share Jesus Christ I run across people all the time who say, 'I don't want to become a Christian, I want to have fun'. Well I want you to know that I haven't met anybody having half the fun I've had. There is more joy in living for Jesus one hour than all the pleasures of a lifetime.

I remember when I first started ministering in California. I met a bunch of the motorcycle riders and I saw the people on the streets, and I was sharing Jesus, but it seemed to conflict. And suddenly I realized that Jesus doesn't turn us off, he turns us around. If you've got the desire to roam around at night, you don't have to go to bed at eight p.m. just because you've become a Christian. You can witness in all places at night. Maybe you've got the spirit in you that you've always wanted to travel. Well, maybe you need to be an evangelist somewhere. Maybe you've the spirit of liking to rough it out in the mountains, camping out and everything. You become a Christian, and you can still do that, except maybe it'll be as a missionary down in the jungles of the Amazon or in the heart of Africa. God doesn't kill our minds when we become a Christian, He opens our heart and brings us into an even larger dimension of living. So when somebody says to you that they want to have fun, say, 'Hey, that's why you want to become a Christian, because there's a joy that only God gives. There's peace, there's direction, there's purpose, there's forgiveness. You can have more fun if you know that when you die you'll be going to heaven, than if you're going to that other place. You can have more fun if you've got God's Spirit in you than if you've got the devil in you, because what God gives you is for real, what the devil gives is a counterfeit and doesn't last.' So share Jesus with joy and enthusiasm.

When Christ was praying, He said, 'I say these things . . . so that they may have the full measure of my joy within them' (Jn. 17.13). God wants His joy in you. Again Jesus said, 'I have come that they may have life, and have it to the full' (Jn. 10.10). He wants us to have an abundant life. And the Bible says, 'If you then . . . know how to give good gifts to your children, how much more will your Father in heaven give the Holy Spirit to those who ask Him!' (Lk. 11.13). God will give you His good gifts. We don't have to be afraid of the will of God. God knows what is best. God knows what will give you more fun and more joy.

The Bible says, 'The way of the transgressor is hard' There is no peace for the wicked. Jesus said, 'Come to me, all you who are weary and burdened, and I will give you rest. Take my yoke upon you and learn from me, for I am gentle and humble in heart, and you will find rest for your souls. For my yoke is easy and my burden is light' (Mt. 11.28, 30). And, 'surely I will be with you always, to the very end of the age'

(Mt. 28.20). I could go on and on, showing you that the Lord gives us more life. God doesn't take away life, He knows how to give you what's best.

DAY 41

Have you ever, as you've witnessed and shared Jesus Christ with somebody, heard, 'But I don't need to become a Christian, I've always been a Christian. I've never needed to repent of my sins and receive Jesus. I was born a Christian, I was confirmed, I was baptized. I was born one'? Do you know that you can't be born a Christian. Everybody who is a Christian has been born the second time. Not just one time in the flesh, but a second time in the Spirit. Listen to the words of God, 'Yet to all who received Him, to those who believed in His name, He gave the right to become the children of God – children born not of natural descent, not of human decision or a husband's will, but born of God' (Jn. 1.12, 13). The only way to be in the family of God is to experience a personal receiving of Jesus in your life. It is a decision that you must make.

But you say to yourselves, what about the children, what about the little babies, are they outside the family of God, will they be separated? Jesus said, 'Let the little children come to me, and do not hinder them, for the Kingdom of heaven belongs to such as these' (Mt. 19.14). And David, the man after God's own heart, said these words when his child died, 'I will go to him, but he will not return to me' (2 Sam. 12.23). The Bible indicates that those who are children are safe in the hands of God. They're in the family of God, by grace, but they still have to be taught to be good; not to be selfish, to give and not to take.

We are all inherently, by nature, distorted and evil, yet at that moment – sometime whenever it is – I don't know, but God knows, and the person knows, God holds us responsible for our life, and at that very moment, we must be willing to receive Him as our Saviour, then we take on the nature of God. So you don't just become a Christian. It must be a wilful decision, whereby you are determined that you want to turn away from living without Jesus, to live your life with Him.

It may be the first time that you ever hear the Gospel. For me, as a child I loved the Lord and I'd been taught about Jesus from the time I was born. The first time that I felt that I was without Jesus I was seven. The first time I realized that I was a sinner and that I needed Jesus to forgive me and save me, I gave my heart to Him. Now at that moment, if I'd said 'no', then I would have been outside of the grace of God because I would have rejected that grace. So, encourage people to receive Jesus, and to be saved through faith in Him.

DAY 42

Many people say, 'What about other religions? Do they need Jesus? Isn't one way as good as any other?' There is a very unique thing about being a Christian. It is different from all other religions of the world. In most religions, except Christianity, it is man's effort to get to God. Whatever the religious viewpoint, it is man doing something to find God; to discover God; to please God. It is man's effort to achieve unity with God. And so basically it is a works' religion, and many people who are involved, even in Christianity, are in the same way. But in Jesus Christ, there is a uniqueness. In Jesus Christ we have God coming to us and doing for us what we could not do for ourself. So in Christianity, we have God seeking to save us and not man seeking to save himself.

I've walked with a cross for many many years around the whole world, on every continent. And as I've gone with the cross into Buddhist countries, Hindu countries, Muslim countries and

Jewish countries, people have seen me with a cross; and maybe there isn't a Christian for miles around, and they come up, and ask what I'm doing. Often I feel that they're going to be antagonistic, but most of the time they're not antagonistic at all. I say that I'm carrying the cross to remind them of the love of Jesus Christ. And most people thousands of miles away in distant lands, ask 'Who is Jesus? I don't know much about him,' or 'I've never heard of him,' or 'I've heard a little about him.' People are interested in Jesus, so I share about Christ.

I don't meet a person of another religion and say instantly that I'm going to convert them, and that they're going to give up being of their faith, and give up their religion, to be a Christian. If I did that, they would start defending their religion, even if they hardly believe in it or didn't practise it. They would just start defending it. But what I say is that 'I want to share about Jesus Christ, who was born and conceived in the womb of Mary by the Holy Spirit, and lived without sin'. And I ask them if they know why He died on the cross. And people often say, 'No, I've wondered about that'. So I explain why He died on the cross, and I share the gospel of Jesus Christ. The message of salvation to everyone who believes. 'Salvation is found in no-one else, for there is no other name under heaven given to men by which we must be saved' (Acts 4.12).

So I talk about the person of Jesus Christ. I talk about the message of the Bible. And if someone says they're of this religion, I say, 'Oh, well, that's wonderful to know that you're interested in your relationship with God.' And I say, 'I just want to show you and tell you a few things about Jesus, because through Him, we can get to know God personally, and He will live in you and be your Saviour forever.' So don't fear, let that fear be cast out.

DAY 43

I'm going to continue sharing about how to witness to people who make objections. Some of us don't witness because we're afraid of what people will say back. God will give you the knowledge of what to do.

As we share Jesus Christ there's frequently someone who says, 'Well, I don't know – I don't need the Lord. I do enough good works. I don't need anything else'. A good Scripture verse to use as a reference is Titus 3.5. But I want to share about good works for a moment, about the person who says, 'I do enough'.

There are many people who give to the church or help the poor; who are kind and do many things that are commendable and good, and yet the Bible teaches that goodness is not enough.

Now when someone says that they do enough, I usually like to say, 'You know, it's very commendable that you do good things. The world needs more people doing good work, but it's not our good works which are going to save us because we've still got a problem, and that problem is called sin'. The Bible says, 'for all who have sinned and fall short of the glory of God' (Rom. 3.23). Our good works may seem good compared to the people around us, but we come short of the goodness of Jesus Christ. When we measure ourselves by Him, we must cry out, 'Woe to me! I am ruined!' (Isa. 6.5). Often I think the thing to say is, 'Let's look at Jesus and how He lived and what He did,' and also, look at the Scripture which says, 'For it is by grace you have been saved, through faith', and 'not by works, so that no-one can boast' (Eph. 2.8, 9). And as we talk about our good works we're saying that what Jesus did, was not good enough. The work of Jesus, when He died upon the cross, is sufficient. That is really all that is needed.

Our goodness is not enough, for all of us have come short of the glory of God. And as we emphasize the righteousness and holiness of Christ, that person can see that their good works are not sufficient to save them. Otherwise, we get involved with trying to put them down. You don't have to try to put anybody down, the devil has already put everybody down. We're to lift everybody up. We're to emphasize what Jesus can do in putting lives together. So if somebody says, 'I do plenty of good works. I don't need Him,' don't start debating or fussing, and saying that you're really bad, just begin to speak about Jesus. Share the truth of the Scripture, and the Holy Spirit of God will show people that they need Jesus.

DAY 44

I tell you, sometimes when I go out witnessing I'll meet people who give me a line like this, 'I enjoy what I'm doing and I don't want to change. I don't want to give it up'. When somebody says something like that I say, 'It's good to have fun, that's why you need to be a Christian. You're interested in life and in the fullness of life. Jesus will give it to you'.

But often, even though we feel good, it doesn't mean that we don't have a problem. A person who feels excellent and goes for his regular yearly check-up, and after the check-up and X-rays the doctor says, 'You have cancer and you're dying', and the guy says, 'Oh, but I feel great, I never felt better in my life.' And the doctor says, 'But you have cancer and you're dying and you need an operation'. The truth sobers, the truth becomes the reality. Sometimes we're under an illusion. How many times has a person drunk poison thinking that it was all right? How many times has a child or an adult been playing with an empty gun, and it was loaded, and says, 'Oh I didn't know'? Their ignorance of the fact did not bring that dead person back to life. There is an affliction we call sin, and sin afflicts everybody. All have sin, and maybe for a moment it doesn't seem too bad, but it is a growth, eating away in a much deadlier fashion than cancer.

The Bible tells us how Moses chose the reproach of Christ rather than the riches of the Pharaoh, 'rather than to enjoy the pleasures of sin for a short time' (Heb. 11.25). Don't ever try and tell somebody that that passage is saying, 'I enjoy. . .' that sometime they don't have any fun at all. The devil has an illusion of fun, he gives an illusion of happiness and pleasure but it is only temporary. If you could just go where I have been, behind the scenes of the neon lights; behind the stages of the night clubs; back where they're hitting up drugs; back where they're committing suicide; back where they're in misery and despair; you'd see that behind the illusion of happiness, there is an emptiness without Jesus Christ. So we need to speak to the heart that pleasure is only for a moment, but God's love is for eternity. And the peace that He gives the world cannot be taken away. The joy that He gives is not for a moment, it is for all eternity. You encourage people to give their lives to Christ, who gives life abundantly, forever.

DAY 45

Let's start off right. Water doesn't make you a fish, does it? Just because you swim doesn't make you a fish; because you drive a car doesn't make you an automobile. Because you go in a barn doesn't make you a mule, does it? Because you go to church, doesn't make you a Christian. Hey, that's heavy, but it's true, isn't it? That's what we often run into when we witness and share about Jesus Christ. There are many people who say, 'Hey, I'm a Christian, I've been baptized. Well, I'm a Christian, I've been confirmed', or 'I joined a church, so therefore I'm a Christian; I'm signed up, it's all right'. But it takes more than that, doesn't it? Jesus said, 'unless a man is born again' (Jn. 3.3). Christ often said that we could clean up the outside so that it looks nice, but inside the cave is full of dead men's bones. It's like a cup that looks clean and beautiful on the outside, but inside it's still full of dirt and grime. So, just because we carry a Bible, doesn't make us a Christian. Just because we can say, 'Praise the Lord' doesn't mean we have the Lord in our heart. Just because we see miracles doesn't mean that we're a Christian. When we stand before the judgement of God, it's not going to mean that we enter heaven just because we cried. You say, 'but Lord, I cried, I remember crying that night, I must be a Christian. Or I remember shouting, I must be a Christian'. No, the only way that a person will be saved is to repent of their sins and receive Jesus Christ into their life as Lord. I mean, to be born of the Spirit. That is what it means to be a Christian.

When people say that they've joined a church, or they're religious, or they've been baptized, don't put them down. That's commendable, that's good but ask them when did they personally repent of their sins and receive Jesus as their Lord. Remember the words of Christ when He said, 'Not everyone who says to me, "Lord, Lord" will enter the Kingdom of Heaven, only he who does the will of my Father who is in heaven. Many will say on that day, "Lord, Lord, did we not prophesy in your name, and in your name drive out demons and perform many miracles?" And the Lord will say, "I never knew you. Away from me, you evildoers!" ' (Mt. 7.21–23).

So it is important that we personally receive Jesus as our Lord, that we know Him. If there was only one thing in this world that you knew for sure, the most important thing to know beyond a shadow of a doubt is that you are saved. And the only way to be saved is through the blood of Jesus. Through the life of Jesus, through his resurrection, and because he lives now. And people can know that, people can receive Jesus. You can know for sure that you are saved, by repenting of your sins and asking Jesus to come into your life to be your Lord. And if you have friends, who need Jesus, show them

John 3.3, or 2 Corinthians 5.17, and read them the 1 John chapter 1, and Revelation 3.20, and invite them to pray with you now.

DAY 46

One of the excuses I hear is, 'Well, I'll wait until I'm older, just before I die, I'll get saved. I want to have a good time and when I get older and settled down, then I'll be ready to trust the Lord'. The person who makes that statement is very foolish, and most people know it when they make it. When somebody tries to lay something like that on me, I kind of laugh and say, 'You know better than that, you know you need the Lord right now'. 'Well, I know I do, but I'm going to wait until I'm older'. Then sometimes I say that I want to share one Scripture verse, which won't take a minute to read, 'Why, you do not even know what will happen tomorrow. What is your life? You are a mist that appears for a little while and then vanishes' (Jas. 4.14). What is your life? It's here for a moment, then it's vanished and gone.

As I've travelled around the world, I've often stopped at cemeteries along the roadside and looked at the tombstones. I like to read the writing on those tombstones. I was in London a while back, and went to Westminster Abbey, to look at the tombstones of people who lived hundreds and hundreds, or almost a thousand years ago, with their names engraved on them. But in most cemeteries the names have peeled off or fallen off and there's no marker. Who is going to remember? – God remembers. He's the only one who is going to remember a long time after you're dead. We don't know how long life is. In my life, I've been with so many people that have died. In car accidents, in the battlefields of the world, people unexpectedly die.

One night I stood on Sunset Strip at the door of our building in Hollywood, and I witnessed to a guy who came in, and I urged him to receive Jesus. And he said, 'Arthur, I'm just about ready to do it. I'll just wait awhile and think about it and I'll come back later tonight'. I said, 'now is the only time. God says this moment, trust Him now, don't put it off.' He said, 'Arthur, I'll be back a little later'. I stood at the door and he walked off, down the street. Half a block away, just a few doors down the street, a guy walked up, stuck a sawed-off shotgun under his chin and blew his head off. Life is short, don't put it off. Urge people to give their lives to Jesus today.

DAY 47

Here's a question that many people have when I start to share Jesus Christ. They'll say, 'Oh, but I know a lot of Christians that aren't living right. They've got problems. Why, I know a Christian who drinks too much. I know a Christian, my next-door neighbour, and they're about to get a divorce. I work with a Christian and the other day he was cursing, he hit his finger and cursed and cursed. No, no, I don't want to be a Christian, too many hypocrites among Christians'.

Christians have got problems just like everybody. Let me share with you. The only perfect Christians are those who have already gone to heaven, do you know that? All the rest of us here on earth are imperfect. But we have a Saviour who is in the business of perfecting us. But just because some Christians have problems that other people refer to and use as an excuse, is not a reason for not being saved. Our salvation does not depend on our faith in other Christians. Our faith must be in Jesus Christ.

When I start to witness people often say, 'Why, I know a preacher who ran off with his secretary, and the treasurer who ran off with all the money. Oh, it doesn't work'. And I say, 'but just one thing, that wasn't Jesus. Jesus talked about the same kind of people'. Everybody is going to stand before the judgement of God. And those Christians are going to be judged by God too. The Bible teaches that many Christians are still carnal ('worldly, mere infants') and God wants to give them the meat of the gospel, but they're still like babies, drinking the milk. God wants to do more with His followers (1 Cor. 3.1–2). Look at the disciples of Jesus, they failed after He had been teaching them for three years, but He didn't give up on them, He kept working to perfect them. So, when somebody says to you that all these Christians have problems, you can say, 'yes, that's true, but I want you to know that Jesus has given victory in my life over many of the things that once defeated me and by His grace and through His strength, I'm going to overcome those things that still cause me problems. But just because I'm weak doesn't mean that Jesus is weak'. 'He is able to save completely, those who come to God through Him' (Heb. 7.25).

When people start talking about weak Christians, I say that there's a bunch of weak ones, but let me talk to you about the one that's strong. The one that overcame. The one that didn't fail, the one that really made it, and His name is Jesus! You'll notice in my teaching about witnessing and the objections which people make, that I basically feel, no matter what question someone asks, start to answer it and then just make a beeline for the cross. Just come right to Jesus and you won't go wrong.

DAY 48

When I begin to witness to someone who says, 'But I don't have the faith, I just don't have the faith', I don't put a person down for saying that, because that's how they feel about it. If they say they don't have it, it isn't an unsurmountable problem. It's a wonderful situation when someone is honest enough to say it. The way I approach it is, if somebody says that they don't have the faith to believe, and they don't have the faith to give their life to God, I say that it's good that they're honest and recognize the need. And since they don't have the faith, I share with them how they can get it. I say, 'if you had the faith, I know you would give your life to the Lord, wouldn't you?' 'Well, if I had it, I guess I would'. 'Okay, let's look at faith'.

The Bible says, 'For it is by grace you have been saved, through faith – and this not from yourselves, it is the gift of God' (Eph. 2.18). God has a gift that He wants to give to everyone, and that gift is the gift of faith. We're saved through faith, it is the gift of salvation, and God gives us the faith to believe. When someone says, 'but how do I get that faith? By asking?' You can say, 'just ask and He'll give you the faith necessary to believe. Now, you know how much faith it takes? It just takes the same amount of faith you already have'. We get in an aeroplane with a pilot we've never seen, we get in a taxi cab with a driver and we don't know how well he can drive, we take a pill from a chemist and we don't know whether it's strychnine or whether it's a vitamin, but we trust that it's labelled correctly. We need to put our faith in God. Put the faith you have and God will give you all the faith necessary.

Here's how it works. Just stop and share with that person. Immediately after you've explained the gospel, have a prayer. I'll ask that person to join me in prayer and I'll pray for them like this, 'Lord, I pray for my brother here that you'll give him the faith that is necessary; that you'll give him the faith to trust in you, and I pray that he'll exercise it for the glory of God'. When I finish praying I say that the person should pray and give that faith to God, using these words, 'Dear God, I give you all the faith I've got, however much or little it is. I believe in Jesus. Come into my heart, save me, change me, make me new. I repent and give my life to God'. Praise God, the Lord will save that person.

So faith is the gift of God. Don't try to generate faith, don't try to brainwash somebody or push them into something. No, God has a gift for them and He will give them the faith necessary. So don't be afraid, share Jesus today and go in the power of the Holy Spirit.

DAY 49

Have you ever been driving down the highway and looked out and seen what appeared to be a beautiful lake of water? Especially those of you who live in desert areas or travel through deserts, have you been confronted with this type of thing? You've looked out and seen a beautiful lake of water but it was all desert. And you say that you don't remember there being a lake on the map. And it wasn't, and the further you drove, the further that lake seemed to move away in front of you. It wasn't water; it was a mirage. It was an illusion; it was not reality.

When you share Christ, you'll encounter a person who says, 'well you see, I don't believe in the Bible, it contradicts itself'. One of several things has happened. Most of the time I find that the person has never really read the Bible, so if you ask them what contradictions, they don't really know. The other thing is that they have read small parts and extracts, but they've not taken it in total context. So what appears to be a contradiction, is not a contradiction at all. It's just an illusion because they they haven't looked at it in its totality.

I have written nine books and many of them are in bookstores now, and as a result, I get letters and people who talk to me all the time who get upset, or something, because they take just a little bit out of one of my books. They open it up and read half a page and get mad and write a letter, but they never read the whole thing. And what they say isn't accurate at all because it's taken out of perspective and out of context. So often, when people say that the Bible is contradictory, it's because they've not read it in the context in which it was written, but have pulled out one verse here and one verse there. The Bible is one message of God. It is God's message of redemption. It reveals our condition; it reveals the work of God to redeem us from the distortion and perversion that the devil has brought into this world; it shows how, once we've received Him as our Saviour, God begins to put our life together and prepare us for heaven; it enlightens us, that we may be whole and complete in our nature. This is the message of God.

The Bible is seeking to convey the message that God loves us, He's interested in us. His spirit is here, He will redeem us and bring us into fullness and ultimately we'll be in His home in heaven. Now, I trust that when somebody says that the Bible contradicts itself, that in the midst of that you'll want to encourage them to study the whole chapter, study the whole book of John or Revelation, or whatever it is, to see what God is saying. There is no contradiction in the Word of God. It is truth, it is accurate, it is God's holy word, and God wants us to understand it. For, 'the man without the Spirit . . . cannot understand them (the things that come from the Spirit of God), because they are spiritually discerned' (1 Cor. 2.14). We need the Holy Spirit to teach us the truth. God will guide you to the truth. Live for Him and share Him.

DAY 50

Have you ever shared with somebody about the Lord and asked about their relationship with Jesus Christ? Or maybe you've asked if they die, do they have the assurance that they would go to heaven? Or you've approached them about Jesus in some way and they've stood back and said that's personal. And that's why I personally ask them about their relationship to the Lord. I'm personally interested in this person. Their relationship with God is a part of my business, because the Father, the one that made us, has given us the responsibility to help each other to live in a pleasing way in His sight. God has given us a commission to be interested in our fellow man, and that's why I can say, 'I am interested in you and I do love you', when witnessing. The reply will be, 'but you don't even know me. How could you love me?' And I say, 'because your Father, the one that made you, loves you and He lives in me, and He wants to give you a new life'. If you just pursue that, you'll find that a person will begin talking to you. Sometimes I've talked to people for an hour about what they didn't want to talk about.

People say that they don't want to talk about religion and politics. And I ask them what it is about religion that upsets them. Usually, they'll just talk for fifteen minutes about why they don't want to talk about religion. And then, I'll just inject Jesus into the conversation, and share about Him. After a while I'll point out that we've been talking about Jesus for forty minutes, which is just the subject they said they didn't want to talk about. Often it's just someone's way of trying to use a little catch-phrase to avoid discussing something they feel uncomfortable about. Sure it feels uncomfortable for a person to talk about Jesus Christ when Satan is reigning in the heart. The old devil gets upset, and he doesn't feel comfortable when the Lord is present. So, understand that.

Sometimes, I'll approach the situation this way. People will say that they don't want to talk about religion and politics. And I'll agree with them, and call it a truce and just talk about Jesus. And they laugh, and say that I'm crazy. And I'll agree, but add that religion won't do them any good, religion will mess them up. You can get religion and you're almost in worse shape than if you had nothing because so often religion has got rules and regulations and everything else and, boy, you feel miserable. You can't have any fun.

But when you have Jesus, you have life. Jesus is different from religion; Jesus is a relationship. He is living. He is alive, and a person can know Him. We have a relationship with God through Jesus Christ.

There's another thing. People will say that they don't want to talk about religion or politics. And I'll say that some of those politicians need a little dose of religion, don't they? And people agree, and they'll start talking about politics like they didn't ever think they would. And I'll say, 'I need a little of Jesus too, don't you think you do?' And I begin to share. See, we've got to love people, share with people; not bash them over the head, but stick out our hand and love. You go forward for Jesus.

DAY 51

Sometimes I meet people who ask this question sincerely, 'Is God really interested in me? I believe there is a God, but I just don't think He's interested in me. If He made this whole planet, and all the universe, and He made all four billion or more people that are on this earth, how could He be interested in me and my problems and my need?' Well, God is God. He is so much greater than we are. And perhaps the best illustration of this is when I met my wife. We met and were married in two weeks and five days. The Bible says, 'Do not quench the Spirit' (1 Thes. 5.19). I love my wife, and that is just wonderful. I also love my mother and my father. And then God blessed us with Ginna, and then Joel, and then Joy, and then Joshua, and then Joseph, and then Jerusalem. So now I'm loving seven in our immediate family, and then my mother is still living and then I have many wonderful friends whom I love. So I love and I have a relationship with many people around the world. Now, God is much, much greater than I am.

God can have a personal relationship and a deep interest in you. The Bible says, 'even the hairs of your head are numbered' (Mt. 10.30). I simply try to understand that God is so much greater, His love is far superior to mine. For God is love. If you said, 'Arthur, how much does God love me?' I'd read you, 'For God so loved the world that He gave His one and only Son, that whoever believes in Him shall not perish, but have eternal life' (Jn. 3.16). If we were to call down the angels from heaven, and say, 'Gabriel, how much does God love us?', all Gabriel, who stands in the very presence of God, could say is 'that God so loved the world that He gave His one and only Son'. You can't add to that. God loves me. God loves you. God loves everybody.

When you're a Christian, you should be filled with God's love, which means that we should love everybody. God said that it's impossible to love Him if we don't love others. We, as believers, should reflect that love. As we witness and tell others about Jesus, they need to know that He loves them, that God cares, and that love is manifest on the cross, in the life that He gave. As you present Jesus Christ to other people, show them that God is interested in them and knows their every need and is able to meet their needs through Jesus Christ.

DAY 52

For the next few days I'm going to share about how you can be an effective witness for Jesus Christ. First of all by looking at your own life, so that Christ can strengthen you and build you up. When a soldier goes out to war, usually he's been through training. Jesus Christ worked with His disciples to teach them and strengthen them so that they would be strong in prayer, and in understanding His word. For you to be an effective witness for Jesus Christ, you need to know the word of God. In the letter to the Ephesians, Paul speaks about us being spiritually prepared by putting on the whole armour of God. You need to have your own life cleansed, and your life filled with the power of the Holy Spirit.

I want to ask you this. Have you let Jesus Christ take control of your life and use you as a witness? Remember Isaiah, who in the very presence of God said, 'Woe to me! I am ruined! For I am a man of unclean lips, and I live among a people of unclean lips' (Isa. 6.5). And God cleansed him, touched his lips and filled him with His power. And he heard God saying, 'Whom shall I send? And who will go for us?' and Isaiah said, 'Here I am. Send me!' (Isa. 6.8). Today, I pray that that will be your commitment to Jesus Christ, that you will let the Lord Jesus fill you and control you and give you boldness.

I want to mention the personal life of anyone who is witnessing, because there's one thing about witnessing, that usually if you continue, God straightens you up. We ought to be clean when we get started, but normally, if we don't know the Bible, witnessing will drive us into it.

I want to share a few points and tips with you about the personal life of the effective, consistent witness. He is the person who is really witnessing because he loves Jesus Christ. Jesus said that if we love Him, we will keep His commandments. We share Christ with others because, like the early believers, we can't help but speak those things which we've seen and heard. So what you need to do is to let God fill you with His love.

Another point is that we really should be living a clean life. If there are things in your life that shouldn't be there, you should repent and let God take them away.

You should be obedient in your own life. You should be actively caring and ministering, in a Bible fellowship and in church. You should be baptized.

Another thing that is very vital to those who are witnessing is that we study the Word of God. The more of God's Bible that we have in our mind, the more effective a reservoir of Scriptures we can use in sharing Christ. Remember, it's 'Not by might nor by power, but by my Spirit, says the Lord' (Zach. 4.6).

Many of you have not witnessed in weeks or months or years. You need to tell somebody about Jesus Christ. You need to come to God today and say, 'Lord, give me your desires. Lord, give me the hunger to win people to Jesus'. Our eyes are dry, we don't weep for the lost, and many of our hearts are cold. Say to the Lord, 'God, awaken me, give me your zeal, your burden, your desire'. Christian, would you pray with me now, 'God, have mercy on me. Forgive me for not being the witness that I should be. Fill me with the power of the Holy Spirit. Set me on fire. Put your words in my mouth and use me as a witness for Jesus Christ'.

DAY 53

As I read and study the Word of God, I become more effective in communicating the love and salvation of Jesus. Every witness for Jesus needs to know the Bible. You need to know what the Scripture says and you need to study the Word of God. The Bible says that we should study to show ourself approved by God. To be an effective witness we need to understand every day – to absorb the spiritual food of the Word.

Sometimes when you start witnessing, people will say that they don't believe the Bible. When they say that to me, most of the time I never answer. I just act like they didn't say it, and I continue sharing about the Scripture. If they come back and repeat that they don't believe the Bible, I say, 'Well, if you don't believe it, it won't hurt you, will it?' And I continue to share what I'm talking about. If they come back a third time and say that they really don't believe the Bible; that it's just another book, I ask them what is there about Romans 6.23, that they don't believe, 'For the wages of sin is death, but the gift of God is eternal life in Christ Jesus our Lord'? Then there we are talking about the Word. Share the Word of God, lift up Jesus and He will draw all men to Himself.

Often I'm asked by people who want to know, outside of what the Bible says, what my opinion is. I say that my opinion is what the Scripture says. The Bible *is* the truth. It does not just contain some truth, but it is *the* truth. It is the Word of God, spoken by God and recorded by man. It is His book, His message to us. We should communicate this message with other people.

So study the Bible, and resolve to eat the Word as your spiritual soul food. And I want to ask those of you who've got a lot of Bibles stacked away at home, to get some of them out that you don't need, and go out on the street and give them away. Give them to somebody; to a friend. You don't need a lot of Bibles in your house, just one good one ought to do you. Give away the Word of God, okay? Study the Word and give away the Word and God will bless you and use you.

DAY 54

I'm happy today to be able to talk about one of my favourite subjects, which is prayer. I remember when I was at Mississippi College and I was searching for power, for the real power of God in my prayer life. As I was praying I tried to imitate everybody I met. I went to some meetings where the preacher would pray looking up and I'd pray looking up; others would pray lying down on the floor; some prayed with their hands up; some prayed with their heads bowed, and some prayed on their knees, and I imitated every single one of these positions in prayer. But I didn't find my prayer life improved by positions. I kept searching and searching, and one time I was in my room, and I said, 'God, what's the key to prayer?' And suddenly it seemed like God gave me this revelation and I felt so foolish. It seemed like the Lord said, 'Arthur, if you want to know how to pray, read Matthew, Mark, Luke and John. And see how I prayed'. Jesus prayed. His prayer life is recorded in the Bible. So I started reading the Scriptures and studying the prayer life of Jesus. Where He went to pray; when He prayed; how much time He prayed; how and what He prayed about, and ever since I've had a desire to pray like Jesus. I want to encourage you to do the same; to look at Jesus Christ and develop your prayer life like His.

The disciples asked the Lord to teach them to pray, and Jesus began by showing them that they needed to say, 'Your will be done on earth as it is in heaven' (Mt. 6.10). Prayer is not you controlling God, but prayer is letting God take control of you. It is allowing Him to put His mind in you. It's not you coming up with a thought and then inviting God to get in on what you're doing, but it is that God already has a plan. He wants to see people saved. He wants you to have the desire that He already has for the unsaved.

Prayer is not only you speaking to Him, but allowing Him to speak to you. We say how we feel and then we need to tune our ears to hear the Spirit of God, so that God's Spirit takes control of our life, so that we're moulded in His image. Every great witness that I've ever met in the world has a deep and vibrant prayer life. You can pray as you drive your car down the street; you can pray in school; you can pray as you wash dishes or work around the house. The Bible says that we should pray without ceasing. If you pray right you'll have the power of God in your life and you'll be an effective witness for Jesus Christ. You'll be able to go anywhere with boldness and tell other people about Jesus. You'll be strong.

Now take your Bible, Matthew, Mark, Luke and John and start looking at the prayer life of Jesus. Underline it in red or something. Study the prayer life of Jesus. Say, 'Lord, I want to pray like you'. Then, 'Your attitude should be the same as that of Christ Jesus' (Phil. 2.5).

DAY 55

I'm continuing to talk about the personal life of the witness for Jesus Christ. It is absolutely essential for an effective witness to be controlled by the Holy Spirit. Many of us have a vocabulary that's spiritual; we know all the terms, but Jesus Christ is not in control of our lives. I want you to know that if you're so full of the Holy Spirit that you've got doves perched on your shoulder, and you're not telling somebody about Jesus, those doves are just crazy. That's not the Holy Spirit. When the Holy Spirit fills your life, He gives you the desire to tell somebody about Jesus. That's what God wants to do with you. He wants to use you and empower you. How do we know? What's the purpose of the filling of the Holy Spirit? 'The fruit of the Spirit is love, joy, peace, patience, kindness, goodness, faithfulness, gentleness and self-control' (Gal. 5.22). Let God take control and give you all that, and you'll be a witness for Jesus.

You hear a lot about the Holy Spirit, but who is He? To be a witness for Jesus, you've got to realize who we're talking about; we're talking about the Spirit of God. God has manifest Himself as Father, as Son, and as Holy Spirit. He is one God. This is His manifestation. The Father loves us. Jesus Christ came into the world from heaven; died on the cross and rose again, and

He's alive and living. God is with us, and Christ is with us through the Holy Spirit. In the air there is oxygen. You don't see it, but it's the power of life. So the spirit of God lives in the believer, and by the power of the Holy Spirit, we have Christ in us. The Spirit of God is at work to bring those who do not know Jesus into His family. You are not the one who convicts somebody of sin or converts them, but it is the Holy Spirit. You allow the Spirit of God to work in you, giving you the Word, and God's Spirit is working on the one that is listening. The Spirit of God convinces and it is the Spirit of God that convicts, and it is the Spirit of God that converts. It is the Spirit of God that converts and keeps the one who trusts Him, in God's family. What we need to do is to allow the Holy Spirit of God to work in our lives. The Holy Spirit is not an it, or a thing. He is alive. He is God. He is God's presence in us. He is at work in you to bring people into the family.

Many of us as believers say that God did a great thing in our life yesterday, or last week or ten years ago, but some of us wonder why we feel kind of empty. Many of us look at our life and wonder what went wrong with the way we were feeling. Have you ever seen a small glass or vase of water which was full? Maybe that was the way it was, comparatively, when you let the Holy Spirit take control of your life, or when you were saved and God filled you. You were full, but then after a few weeks or months, you were searching and felt like something was wrong and didn't know what had happened. God took the little vase that was full and enlarged your capacity, and having enlarged your capacity, with the original amount of water, your vase is just half full. You need to be constantly filled with the Holy Spirit. You need to grow constantly in the Lord. You need to grow in your witness, in your walk in the Spirit. God gives you something and until you give it away by telling somebody else about Jesus, you can't grow any more. You've got to exercise the faith God gives you, then you have the capacity to move on and on and on. Many of us Christians get kind of discouraged when we see the troubles around us, and so many problems in the world, and it looks like so many people need Christ. As a reaction, start another prayer meeting, or another Bible study. We dig a little hole in which we're moaning and groaning, saying, 'God, save the world. God, do something. God, help us'. I think sometimes God gets so sick, He wants to say, 'Shut up – get out, and do something!'

DAY 56

Oh, praise the Lord! I'm having a wonderful time sharing. Today I'll look at a Scripture verse which is to do with what God wants to do, to make us more productive for His glory. Listen to these words, 'He cuts off every branch in me that bears no fruit, while every branch that does bear fruit he trims clean so that it will be even more fruitful. I am the vine; you are the branches. If a man remains in me and I in him, he will bear much fruit; apart from me you can do nothing' (Jn. 15.2, 5).

God's purpose is that we bear fruit, but the only way to bear fruit is for a tree to be pruned. A tree must be cut back, it must be clipped off to allow new growth, and it is the new growth that bears fruit. Therefore, there must be a cutting back. Many of us Christians need to be pruned by God, and sometimes that pruning is painful. Often when you see a skilled man who is pruning a tree, an onlooker might think that he is killing the tree, cutting off those beautiful branches and cutting it back and back and back. But out of that issues new growth, and that's where the fruit comes. And so it is with our lives. God must cut us back. Many of us get involved in worldly things. We get more involved and interested in ball games, or the stock market, or in anything, and as we get involved in the things of the world, we lose interest in the spiritual things of God. God has to prune us back.

Many of us have to be pruned by God because we get involved in spiritual activities or religious activities. Back and forth to the church; coming and going, to hear this evangelist, this singer, but we're not bearing any fruit, all we're doing is becoming parasites of the Kingdom of God. Wanting good music, wanting good sermons, and burning up gas that we should never have, and we're never sharing Christ. And so God needs to prune us and cut us back as He wants us to bear fruit. The Bible says, 'If a man remains in me and I in Him, he will bear much fruit' (Jn. 15.5).

God wants you to bear a lot of fruit. He doesn't want you to be a plant that grows up and looks pretty and then bears no fruit. As Jesus said, 'If anyone does not remain in me, . . . such branches are picked up, thrown into the fire and burned' (Jn. 15.6). God will only keep the plant that bears fruit. God is wanting you to be fruitful. God is wanting your life to bear others into the Kingdom of God. Be filled with the Spirit and from your life, go forth in the power of Jesus today.

DAY 57

It is so good to know that all the time Jesus Christ lived, He truly communicated to the heart and not only to the mind. He spoke in words and in language that people about Him understood. In Matthew chapter 13, we see Christ relating the whole gospel message to a thing as small as a seed, as He tells the famous parable of the sower. Some seeds fell on stony places and some on soft soil, and they sprang up, and some withered away when it got hot. Jesus was speaking to farmers who knew that way of life.

I grew up on a farm in Louisiana, and I have many terms that I used as a child which I don't use out on the Sunset Strip in Hollywood, because many people don't know those terms. Our vocabulary on that cotton farm in Louisiana is different from the vocabulary of Hollywood's Sunset Strip. So in my own life I use words that vary from place to place. I don't use the same words in the African Bush, or the South American jungles, as I do in a big city in Central America, or in London or Paris. We must communicate the gospel in a way people understand, because many people growing up in the city find it hard to understand some of the terms in the Bible.

Sometimes critics get upset because I'll say things like 'turn on to Jesus'. And I know when

I preach on the Sunset Strip, where I often preach, I'll be saying things like, 'Hey, if you wanna get high, you don't have to drop acid, all you gotta do is pray and you go all the way to heaven. If you wanna get loaded, you don't hafta load up on downers or pills, just drop a little Matthew, Mark, Luke and John, and God will get it together in your heart and in your mind. Turn on to Jesus, He is an eternal rush, He'll get your trip together. Get your act together, man, and get right with God now'. Now, those words sound like terms that some of you don't understand, but the guys and girls that I work with in Hollywood, they understand, just as clear as Jesus speaking of seeds and farming. The Bible truth is real.

Jesus met people where they were and when He met Nicodemus, who began to intellectualize about how he could be born again, Jesus spoke about the wind, and He spoke about the Spirit, and He spoke about birth, because here was an intellectual trying to figure things out. And Jesus brought him back to simplicity. He spoke in such a way that the man understood what He was saying. So let us share Christ in fullness, and in words that people understand. Go and meet someone today, and share Jesus with them.

DAY 58

Good news! I love you! And better news than that, Jesus loves you! And that's the best news in all the world. God loves us all even though many of us are unlovely, and that is the good news that Christians share in witnessing to the world. We are Jesus' representatives and so we are to love people, not just to love 'the soul' but all of that person. We're to be interested in people. Jesus loved people. The Bible tells us, 'A man with leprosy came to Him and begged Him on his knees, "If you are willing, you can make me clean" ' (Mk. 1.40). Now, by law, a leper was supposed to stay away from those who did not have leprosy. Lepers had to stand at a great distance and cry, 'unclean, unclean', but this man, breaking all law and tradition, rushed up to Jesus and fell at His feet and looked up, with a hand and face distorted by leprosy, and said, 'If you are willing, you can make me clean', and Jesus, 'Filled with compassion, reached out His hand and touched him' (Mk. 1.41). I don't think that Jesus reached out just a little finger and touched him, I feel that He put His arm around him, and He hugged him right up close, and He said, 'I am willing. Be clean!' Immediately the leprosy left him and he was cured (Mk. 1.42). Jesus is interested in our needs and He loves us. Even though we may be physically unlovely, even though spiritually we may be unlovely, He has the power to make us whole, and you can experience that life-changing power of Jesus Christ. But as a Christian, this is the Jesus that you represent.

Sometimes we meet a person who may be obviously drunk; a wino or an alcoholic, somebody who is lying on the curb in their own vomit, and as a loving Christian, you should genuinely care. You should want to sit down there by them, lift them up, help clean them up, sober them up, minister to them and give them the life of Jesus Christ. That's what God wants from you, to use you to transmit His love.

One time I was witnessing and carrying the cross, in Africa, and I had an interpreter. The interpreter loved God and he loved the Word. He was driving in front of me as I walked with the cross, and crowds would gather and he would interpret as I preached. And I noticed something very strange, as soon as I finished preaching, he was ready to get in the Land Rover and drive off. He didn't even want to touch the people. What he wanted was to be able to preach somehow, but not be involved with touching the diseased skins and sick bodies. Sometimes I think that's the way it is with some of us who love God. We love the Word, but wc don't love others, and that's what we need to do. To love other people with all of our heart, all of our soul, all of our strength, and let God's love flow through us to other people. When Jesus was here, He touched the lepers; he let the sinner woman wash His feet; He washed the disciples' feet. As you witness, be sensitive, and allow God to fill you with His love for people, so that His pure love reaches out and touches them.

DAY 59

Let's look at how Jesus was interested and sensitive, and approached an opportunity to change a man's life. The Bible says in Mark chapter 10 that there was a blind man named Bartimaeus who was sitting by the highway begging, and he heard that Jesus Christ was coming by. And when he heard this, he began to scream, 'Jesus, Son of David, have mercy on me!' and 'Many rebuked him and told him to be quiet', but the man cried out all the more, and then, the Bible says, 'Jesus stopped' (Mk. 10.47–49). The religious leaders who were Jesus' associates wanted Him to move on, 'Here's a heckler, here's a guy that is going to cause problems', and yet Jesus saw him and loved him, and said, 'What do you want me to do for you?' and the blind man said, 'Rabbi, I want to see'. 'Go,' said Jesus, 'your faith has healed you. Immediately he received his sight and followed Jesus along the road'

(Mk. 10.51, 52). Isn't this a wonderful story, about how Christ was there, and was interested in that man, and in his needs.

I was in Portugal one day, and as I was walking along the road, I saw a bus on the roadside and a mass of tourists pouring out of it. I knew they were tourists because they had so many cameras. And because they had their cameras, they were taking pictures of a poor old lady with a huge pot on her head. I saw them taking pictures of that lady, and they soon saw me, and came rushing over and said, 'You're brother Blessitt with your cross. Why, this is the highlight of our trip. We want to take a picture.' And I refused because I'm not a slide. They had just seen a woman who was suffering. She was carrying a huge load on her head and they didn't give her a prayer, a tract or a Bible. They didn't help her with her load; offer her money; nothing, but just took pictures. And I thought, oh my, that's what many of us have done. We've only photographed the world. We haven't gone into the world. We have too many tourist Christians, and God wants us to be involved.

DAY 60

Oh Praise the Lord! The joy of the Lord is my strength! And it is such a joy to live for Jesus Christ and to serve Him and walk with Him in our lives. It's important for us to get started in serving the Lord Jesus Christ. On Christmas Day, 1969, I took one step that was very significant. It didn't seem like a very big step but it was a step forward from Hollywood, California toward Washington D.C., carrying a twelve foot cross on my shoulder. Now that first step didn't get me to Washington, but I would have never made it to Washington if I hadn't taken that first step. And now, years and years have passed, and I've walked 19,000 miles with that cross across every continent in 59 countries, and if I hadn't taken that first step and begun, I would never have made it around the world.

Many people have shared with me about talking about Jesus, because they've had the desire to. God's Spirit has been stirring them, but they've got to take that first step of witness in order to be the kind of person God wants us to be. Many of us have said, 'If I knew how to witness like you do, or if I could preach like Billy Graham or something, I'd be out there doing it, but I don't know, I don't have the experience, and I don't know what to say'. But the key thing is to begin; 'Not by might, nor by power, but by my Spirit, says the Lord' (Zech. 4.6). The beautiful thing about the Bible is how it tells the truth.

The early disciples weren't any more experienced in witnessing than you are. I dare say you've heard a lot more of the gospel than those early Christians because you've been hearing it for years. It was new to them, and yet Jesus took them and trained them and not only that, but in the book of Acts, we find other people who had never met Jesus; except in their heart as their Saviour, who began to witness and share their faith.

So reach out and go for God. There is a mighty harvest that is taking place in this world. God is pouring out his Spirit today in a fresh and mighty way. Not with bought or commercialized evangelism, but just by using people, like you; men, women, and young people. So begin sharing Christ today.

Now you say, 'But Arthur, I wish I had a group'. Then start the group. When I was in college, and through the whole of my life, I've got together one, two or three guys or girls and we'd go out together. So get your own group. You be a kind of captain of a group and say, 'John, Joe, Bill, Mr. Smith, Mr. Jones, let's go out witnessing in our neighbourhood, or downtown, or where ever it is the Spirit of God leads you.

Get started, get together, pray together, witness together, and go out into the world. And if there is anything I can do to help you, just drop me a note. I'll send you gospel tracts, Jesus stickers, and share with you in any way I can; to help you get out there, moving for God. Truly, the fields are ripe for harvest. Now is the time, today is the day of salvation. Share Jesus Christ with somebody today, not tomorrow, today. Get out and let's get going for God!